MASTERING

TYPEWRITING

CW00471676

MACMILLAN MASTER SERIES

Banking	Hairdressing
Basic Management	Italian
Biology	Keyboarding
British Politics	Marketing
Business Communication	Mathematics
Chemistry	Modern British History
COBOL Programming	Modern World History
Commerce	Nutrition
Computer Programming	Office Practice
Computers	Pascal Programming
Data Processing	Physics
Economics	Principles of Accounts
Electronics	Sociology
English Grammar	Spanish
English Language	Statistics
English Literature	Study Skills
French	Typewriting Skills
French II	Word Processing
German	

OTHER BOOKS BY PAUL BAILEY

Comprehensive Keyboard
Comprehensive Typing (2nd edition)
Mastering Keyboarding
Mastering Office Practice
Typing Task Books (comprising Typing Problems; Letters, Postcards and
    Memoranda; Displays and Tabulations)
Typing for Colleges 1 (revised edition)
Typing for Colleges 2 – Typewriting and Communication (2nd edition)
Typing for West Africa
Typing for East Africa

MASTERING
TYPEWRITING SKILLS

PAUL BAILEY

MACMILLAN

First published 1984
Reprinted 1985

Published by
Higher and Further Education Division
MACMILLAN PUBLISHERS LTD
Houndmills, Basingstoke, Hampshire RG21 2XS
and London
Companies and representatives
throughout the world

Printed in Hong Kong

British Library Cataloguing in Publication Data
Bailey, Paul, 1937 Dec 29–
Mastering typewriting skills – (Macmillan master
series)
1. Typewriting
I. Title
652.3   Z49
ISBN 0–333–35104–5
ISBN 0–333–35105–3 [export]

CONTENTS

CONTENTS

CONTENTS

PREFACE

One of the great modern myths is the notion that now that we are in the age of the word processor, memory typewriter or microcomputer with a word processing program the traditional typist's skills are no longer relevant. *Mastering Typewriting Skills* has been written to bridge the gap between the old and new technology: to give those with a traditional typewriter an insight into the new technology, and those with the new technology a sound knowledge of all forms of layout relevant to all the elementary and intermediate public typewriting examinations. The book has been written with the needs of those seeking public examination qualifications and those who simply want to know how to type for their own personal, business or social use in mind.

Mastering Typewriting Skills assumes that the reader has a keyboarding knowledge as defined in my *Mastering Keyboarding*. Using step-by-step instructions suitable to users of typewriters or word processors the text covers the syllabuses of all the elementary and intermediate public examinations. (The syllabuses of the advanced examinations are covered in my *Typing for Colleges 2 – Typewriting and Communication.*) After a full explanation of each subject area the reader is given worked examples before being provided with suitable exercises. The text covers an extremely wide subject area and is written with the needs of the home user in mind as well as those of the examinations student. There are sections on duplicating, the production of business documents and documents connected with the running of meetings as well as manuscript/typescript preparation, the production of accounts, plays and poetry, while the usual examination subjects such as letters, envelopes, postcards, memorandums, forms, paragraphing, headings, displays, tabulations, standard and manuscript abbreviations, correction signs, continuation sheets, etc., are fully covered.

The text does not seek to teach the reader how to use a word processor but merely to give guidance as to word processing functions. All word processors and microcomputers with a word processing program operate in different ways and the user will need to follow the machine manual or be given specific instruction for the system being used. *Mastering Typewriting Skills* points the reader to the relevant sections of the manuals so that they can 'graft on' typewriting skills to the mechanical process involved in operating such equipment. A glance at the index will indicate the degree to which the new technology is written into this text.

PREFACE

The author acknowledges the support of his editor, Margaret Bailey, without whose patience and understanding this text would not have been completed.

PAUL BAILEY

INTRODUCTION:

USING THIS BOOK

This text assumes that you have mastered keyboarding as defined in my *Mastering Keyboarding*, and that you have access to the typewriter, word processor or word processing manual/program to be used. Before starting the text you should work out your aims, i.e. what you would like to achieve at the end of your period of study. If you simply want to learn to type for your own interest and enjoyment, you should list those topics you want to learn about. If you want to take a public examination in typewriting or word processing you should obtain the relevant syllabus from the examining body whose examination you hope to take. (If you are attending an education establishment your teacher or lecturer will tell you the syllabus.) Once you have a list of those items you want/need to cover, match them to the contents of this book before following the topics in the order in which they are introduced. If you followed *Mastering Keyboarding* you can ignore Chapter 1.

Each chapter contains all the teaching material you will require to master each subject area. After following the worked examples you should attempt the exercises which follow.

Many public examinations offer speed tests and one way of preparing for these is to practise typing a range of material. The syllabuses will give details of speed tests – the time given and the amount of material to be typed. You should regularly select samples of the teaching material or the exercises in this book and type them for the time allowed in the public examinations. As a general rule you should aim to type with one error or less for each minute of timing. Analyse your production faults and use The Clinic from *Mastering Keyboarding* to correct them.

All public examinations are, really, a test of output, and once you have followed the required topics in this book you should obtain copies of past examination papers and try to type them in the time allowed. The length and style of public typewriting examination varies from authority to authority but most require an *output speed* of between 6 and 11 standard words per minute, though many syllabuses talk of a *typing speed* of between 25 and 50 words per minute. Some examination authorities publish guides indicating how papers are to be marked and these can assist your examinations preparation.

INTRODUCTION

For those who simply want 'to learn to type' this text offers practical advice on such topics as private and business correspondence, agendas, minutes, plays, poetry, manuscript preparation and duplicating. The ability to produce accurate and well laid out material economically is a valuable asset to all typists and word processor users.

If, having completed this book, you want to take the advanced typewriting examinations or to learn a little more about the subject you should read my *Typing for Colleges 2 – Typewriting and Communication*. The text includes full speed and accuracy development and The Clinic for the diagnosis and correction of typing faults.

THE DIVISION OF WORDS AT THE RIGHT-HAND MARGIN

Those who have worked through *Mastering Keyboarding* will know that some electronic typewriters and all word processors or microcomputers with a word processing program can produce a *justified right-hand margin* by increasing the spaces between words or punctuation marks in a line when the justification control is in operation. If you are using a typewriter without this facility or you want to produce work with a *ragged right-hand margin* and you are using a word processor you will need to know how to divide words at the right-hand margin. This is particularly true if you are using a word processor and you want to re-form paragraphs.

1.1 TO DIVIDE WORDS AT THE RIGHT-HAND MARGIN

On a typewriter the following apply:

1. Listen for the bell or buzzer and see how many spaces there are after it before the margin stop. Do not divide words of this length. If up to 3 letters of a word remain use the margin release key to 'go through' the margin and finish the word. The margin release key operates for one line at a time only.
2. Never divide a word which begins with a capital letter unless the word is hyphenated, in which case divide where the hypen occurs, e.g. Capel-y-ffin.
3. Never divide a word of one syllable or its plural, e.g. bounce(s).
4. Never divide abbreviations, numbers, sums of money, courtesy titles and numbers from the word to which they refer, e.g. FRIBA, 890 500, $250 350, Mrs Sommerfield, 23 Ash Hill, 16 December 1982.
5. Do not divide before 2 letters or after only one, e.g. operat(ed), (f)licker.
6. Do not divide on more than 2 consecutive lines.

1.2 IF YOU MUST DIVIDE A WORD

1. Place the hyphen directly after the first part of the word you are dividing.
2. Divide between syllables so that the pronunciation of the word being divided is understood from the first line, e.g. grue-some.
3. Divide at the hyphen if the word is hyphenated, e.g. eight-day.
4. Divide between repeated consonants, e.g. neces-sary.
5. Divide before 'ing', e.g. discount-ing, except where the final consonant of a word is doubled for the addition of 'ing', in which case divide between the double consonant, e.g. refer-ring.

Do not divide:

> the last word in a paragraph;
> the last word on a page;
> foreign words – unless you know what they mean and where to divide them.

Some authorities consider that time spent obtaining a reasonably straight right-hand margin is time wasted and the modern trend is not to divide words unless it is unavoidable. Many modern electronic typewriters have an *automatic carriage return facility* which decides when to return the printing head and so the user is able to concentrate on entering material with no thought as to the division of words at the right-hand margin. Word processors or microcomputers with a word processing program also have this 'wrap round' facility. When using the latter machines and you want to *re-form paragraphs* – for example, when you decide to change the length of the printing line – you should follow the manual instructions. You may well find that when doing this the machine will ask if you want to divide words by inserting the hyphen or whether you want the whole of the word to appear on the next line. If the work is to be produced with a justified right-hand margin you will probably opt not to divide words, while if the work is to be produced with a ragged right-hand margin you may decide that you want to keep the margin reasonably straight by dividing words. On manual machines and some electric/electronic type-writers you have no choice – the machine will only produce a ragged margin, unless you are prepared to spend a great deal of time manually adjusting the printing line. The manual for your machine will tell you how to do this.

PARAGRAPHS AND HEADINGS

Paragraphs are used to break up matter into distinct sections and 3 kinds are used: *blocked* (sometimes called *flush*), *indented* and *hanging*.

2.1 BLOCKED PARAGRAPHS

Blocked paragraphs are those in which all the lines begin at the same point on the left, usually at the left-hand margin. Some people call these paragraphs *flush paragraphs* because all the lines begin flush or straight on the left. See page 8 for an example of a passage with blocked paragraphs.

When producing *blocked paragraphs* in *single line spacing* turn up 2 single lines to leave one blank line between them. When producing *blocked paragraphs* in *double line spacing* turn up 2 'double' lines to leave 3 blank lines between them.

If you are using *line-and-a-half spacing* and you are producing blocked paragraphs *return the carriage twice.* If you are using a machine with a Visual Display Unit (VDU) you will not be able to see line-and-a-half spacing on the screen – you will only be able to see single or double line spacing on it. You should consult your manual for the coding instructions for printing in line-and-a-half spacing.

2.2 INDENTED PARAGRAPHS

Indented paragraphs are those in which the *first line only* is set in from the left margin – all other lines in the paragraph begin at the left margin. It is usual to start the first line half an inch in from the margin which means *5 spaces pica* (10 pitch), *6 spaces elite* (12 pitch) or *8 spaces* when using 15 pitch. Some authorities allow an indent of 5 spaces for both pica (10 pitch) and elite (12 pitch) while others accept any consistent indents up to $1\frac{1}{2}$ in (38 mm). You are advised to keep to 5 spaces pica, 6 spaces elite and 8 spaces 15 pitch. You must be consistent within any piece of work.

In typewriting, the amount of space occupied by each letter or character is measured in terms of fractions of an inch – 10 pitch taking up 1/10 in; 12 pitch 1/12 in and 15 pitch 1/15 in. When *proportional spacing* is used, the basic measurement is 1/60 in and each character occupies a different amount of space although for the purpose of margins manufacturers often state that the head is 10 pitch or 12 pitch – the information is stamped on the head. Typing paper (see Appendix B) is measured in metric units and there is no exact conversion to fractions. In typewriting, 1 in is taken to be 25 mm and $\frac{1}{2}$ in is taken to be 13 mm.

When producing *indented paragraphs* in *single line spacing* turn up 2 single lines to leave *one blank line* between them. When producing indented paragraphs in *double line spacing* turn up one 'double' line to leave one blank line between them – the same as for single line spacing.

When using *line-and-a-half spacing* return the carriage/head once on a typewriter. If you are using a VDU you will not be able to see line-and-a-half spacing and you should consult your manual for printing instructions.

Use the tabulator (see Appendix A) to save time when typing indented paragraphs – set it at the point at which you want to start each first line. If you are using a word processor consult the manual. See page 9 for an example of a passage with indented paragraphs.

2.3 HANGING PARAGRAPHS

Hanging paragraphs are those in which the first line only begins at the left margin. All other lines start 2 or 3 spaces (consistently) in from the left margin. You are advised to use an inset of 2 spaces when producing hanging paragraphs. If you are using a typewriter, set a tab 2 spaces in from the left margin to save time when typing hanging paragraphs. The alternative is to set a tab for the start of the first line and a left margin for the body of the paragraph. Use the margin release key and the tabulator to find the starting point of each new hanging paragraph. If you are using a word processor you should consult the manual – the method of operation varies from machine to machine.

When producing *hanging paragraphs* in *single line spacing* turn up 2 single lines to leave a blank line between them. When producing them in *double line spacing* turn up one 'double' line to leave a blank line between them – as for single line spacing. When using *line-and-a-half spacing* return the carriage *once* on a typewriter. If you are using a machine with a VDU consult your manual for printing instructions. You will only be able to see the work in single or double line spacing on the screen. See page 10 for an example of a passage with hanging paragraphs.

Hanging paragraphs are usually used when producing lettered or numbered sections.

2.4 EASE OF REFERENCE

For ease of reference all kinds of paragraphs may be numbered or lettered and the numbering may be with arabic numbers (1, 2, 3, etc.) or Roman numerals (i, ii, iii, etc.), while decimal notation is often used, particularly with minutes. See pages 18, 19 and 24 for examples.

2.5 INSETTING

In general material, sections may be inset to draw attention to them. The left margin is brought in for the section(s) to be emphasised – usually by 13 mm ($\frac{1}{2}$ in) – 5 spaces pica, 6 spaces elite or 8 spaces 15 pitch – although any consistent number of spaces is acceptable to many authorities. Some authorities prefer that if the left margin is inset the right margin is inset as well. The inset sections may be produced in the blocked, indented or hanging style – irrespective of the style of the rest of the material, though some authorities do not like hanging insets with generally.blocked material. See page 11 for an exercise with inset paragraphs.

2.6 HEADINGS

Headings are used to label work for ease of reference and headings may be used before material or within it.

Main heading

A main heading tells the reader what the work which follows is about. In general material the main heading is produced at the left margin when using blocked or hanging paragraphs; centred over the printing line when using indented paragraphs.

A main heading should be produced in CAPITAL LETTERS with one or 2 spaces between each word. You are advised to keep to one space between words for economy. A main heading may be underscored. See page 243.

Sometimes a main heading is produced in S P A C E D   C A P I T A L S – a space is left between each letter and *3 spaces* are left between each word. It is not usual to underscore a heading in spaced capitals – though this is acceptable to some authorities. See also Appendix C.

If a piece of work has only one heading – a main heading – turn up 2 or 3 single lines before starting the rest of the work. Some authorities insist on 2 blank lines (turn up 3 single lines) after a main heading.

To centre a heading over the printing line when using indented paragraphs see page 239.

Sub-heading

A sub-heading adds something to the information supplied by the main heading. It is produced in the same position as a main heading. If there is a sub-heading turn up 2 single lines after the main heading (thus leaving one blank line between the main heading and the sub-heading). If the sub-heading goes on to more than one line leave a blank line (turn up 2 single lines) between each line of sub-heading. Turn up 2 or 3 single lines after the last line of a sub-heading before producing the body of the material which follows – some authorities insist on 2 blank lines (turn up 3 single lines) between the last line of a heading and the material which follows.

Sub-headings are usually produced with an initial capital letter and are underscored. See pages 8–18 for exercises.

Shoulder heading

A shoulder heading is produced at the left margin, no matter what the style of the paragraph under it, one blank line above the paragraph which follows (turn up 2 single lines). Shoulder headings may be produced with an initial capital letter (in which case they must be underscored) or all in capitals (in which case they need not be underscored). No matter what style you adopt you must be consistent within any piece of work. See page 12–13 for exercises.

Paragraph heading

A paragraph heading leads into a paragraph and, like the shoulder heading and sub-heading, tells the reader a little more about what is to follow. Paragraph headings may be used in conjunction with shoulder headings and they can be produced in several forms:

(i) as closed capitals (the first words may be in capital letters with one space between each word) with or without underscore
(ii) with an initial capital letter (in which case they must be underscored)
(iii) run into the paragraph (they appear as the first words in the paragraph)
(iv) followed by a full stop or a colon.

Paragraph headings may be used with blocked, indented or hanging paragraphs. See pages 14–15 for exercises.

Side (marginal) headings

Called *side headings* by some authorities and *marginal headings* by others, these headings are set in the left margin and are distinct from the body of the material to which they refer. They may be used in conjunction with shoulder headings. These headings may be produced with an initial capital letter or all in capital letters and in either case they may be underscored. Long side (marginal) headings may be produced on more than one line in single line spacing and they may be used in conjunction with blocked, indented or hanging paragraphs. Side (marginal) headings should not be punctuated unless the last word is abbreviated and standard punctuation is being used. You are advised to leave 3 spaces between the longest side (marginal) heading in a piece of work and the material which follows. *On a typewriter* from the left margin *either*

tap out on the space bar once for each letter and space in the longest line of the side heading and 3 spaces to set a tab for the body of the material

or

set a tab at the left margin position and move the left margin in one space for each letter and space in the longest line in the side heading and 3 spaces between it and the body of the material which follows and reset the left margin. Use the margin release key to 'go through' the left margin to type the side headings.

When using a word processor you should follow your manual's instructions. See pages 16–17 for exercises.

2.7 NUMBERED AND LETTERED PARAGRAPHS

As indicated earlier, numbers or letters may be used to indicate sections within material (see page 24 for decimal notation). When using either numbers or letters they may be:

(i) produced inside the paragraph to which they refer (see page 20)
(ii) produced outside the paragraph to which they refer (see page 19)
(iii) bracketed on the right only (see page 20)
(iv) bracketed on both sides (see page 21)
(v) left unbracketed – especially when produced outside the paragraph to which they refer (see page 22)

Do not mix styles within any piece of work. See pages 18–22 for exercises.

8

Exercise 1

Practise blocked (flush) paragraphs with main and sub-headings – see page
3. Use single line spacing. **Margins**: left 38 mm (1½ in); right 25 mm (1 in).
(See page 36.) Keep your own right-hand margin as straight as possible if
you are using a typewriter – justify it if you are using a word processor.

FLOPPY DISKS

What they are

Floppy disks are part of the micro scene and, for most people,
they are a normal everyday tool which can be used at home and
at work alike. They are the modern equivalent of files – a
media on which the information used in microcomputers is kept.

A floppy disk is, essentially, a thin plastic disk coated with
iron oxide (the coating used on many hi-fi cassettes). Just
as you store information on tapes so do you store information
on floppy disks. What you store you can play back – and if
you get tired of what you have stored you can record over it.
Instead of a long length of tape a floppy disk has circles
coded on to its surface and, just like a long-playing record,
the wider the circle the more information is stored. It
follows that the outside areas of disks store more information
than those nearer the centre.

The recording head on the disk drive of a micro (which also
serves as a playing head) slides along the top of the disk and
to prevent friction and wear minute quantities of special
grease are applied to the surface of the disk. To prevent
damage to that part of the disk not open to the head at any
one time the whole is encased in a cardboard envelope. This
envelope keeps dust and grease (from fingers) off the disk.

Disks should not be used in a smoky atmosphere or one which
is at all dusty because like long-playing records they are
soon damaged by dust of any kind. Again like long-playing
records, the surface of disks is slightly worn away by the
head each time they are used and a bouncing head can cause as
much damage as a bouncing stylus. To prevent loss of vital
information users should keep three copies of each disk and
update this information regularly.

Exercise 2

Practise an article with indented paragraphs and a main and a sub-heading – see page 3. Use single line spacing. **Margins**: left 38 mm ($1\frac{1}{2}$ in); right: 25 mm (1 in). (See page 36.) Keep your right-hand margin as straight as possible if you are using a typewriter – justify it if you are using a word processor.

WORD PROCESSING

Two approaches

A word processor is a term generally used to describe a mechanical or electronic device used in the handling of words which go to make up texts. These texts can be changed and adapted in a number of ways prior to printing and the changes, adaptations and printing can be done at high speed. In short a word processor is a tool used to speed up a process which would take a long time if done manually. It is worth remembering that the world managed for thousands of years without word processors but, like many modern inventions, they make life easier (if correctly used).

Manufacturers of word processing machines have tended to approach the problem from two starting points. Those who were involved in the production of typewriters approached the problem by being concerned with the manipulation of the tools of English Language (for English read French, German, etc as appropriate) and the basic tools of language are the letters of the alphabet, words, phrases, sentences – and so on. These manufacturers were concerned only with the manipulation of words – the origination, manipulation and final production of words in hard copy (printed copy). They were aware of the conventions used in typewriting and how the typewriter related to the office situation in particular.

Manufacturers of microcomputers approached the problem of word processing almost by accident. They were concerned with the production of a tool which could store, manipulate, re-order and collate any kind of information before presenting it as hard copy. Machines which could handle scientific and mathematical data naturally found that language was just another problem and today there is very little difference between a dedicated word processor and a microcomputer with a word processing program and a printer.

Exercise 3

Practise an article with hanging paragraphs and a main and a sub-heading
– see page 4. Use single line spacing. **Margins**: left 38 mm (1½ in); right:
25 mm (1 in). (See page 36). Keep your right-hand margin as straight as
possible. If you are using a word processor, use a ragged right-hand margin.

SAVINGS

How to make them work in the United Kingdom

People fortunate enough to be able to save in the United
Kingdom have a range of options open to them. Of these the
following are the most readily available to the 'man in the
street'.

1   The Post Office has branches in most towns and villages
        and so is very accessible. With just £1.00 to open an
        account there is the option of an Ordinary account or an
        Investment account. The former allows some tax free
        interest while the latter is all taxable. Current rates
        of interest can be found at any Post Office. Money is
        available from an Ordinary account on demand (there is a
        limit on how much can be drawn out at any given time)
        but with an Investment account you have to wait a month.

2   The Joint Stock Banks (sometimes called The Big Four –
        Midland, Barclays, Nat/West and Lloyds) offer Deposit
        accounts (for savers with a minimum of £1.00) and
        Savings accounts for savers who want to save a regular
        sum each month. All interest is taxable. There are
        branches of one or more of the Joint Stock Banks in most
        towns but opening hours are not so convenient as The
        Post Office.

3   Building Societies help house buyers by lending them money
        which they have offered to keep (at interest) for
        savers. They offer a range of accounts and they pay the
        tax due on the interest they pay. For tax payers they
        have an attraction and there are branches of the many
        building societies in most towns and villages – with the
        attraction of Saturday morning opening.

4   The Trustee Savings Bank will accept sums both large and
        small but the interest paid is taxable.

Exercise 4
Practise insetting – see page 5. Use single. line spacing. **Margins**: left
38 mm (1½ in); right 25 mm (1 inch). (See page 36). If you are using a
typewriter, keep your right-hand margin as straight as possible. If you are
using a word processor, use a ragged right-hand margin. Inset both left and
right margins 13 mm (½ in). Note the use of spaced capitals in the main
heading – see page 5.

M O N E Y

Legal tender and near money

Many individuals are not aware of the differences between
what the legal expert calls 'legal tender' and what the
businessman uses as money subsitutes. Any payments can be
made with legal tender but other methods, such as cheques and
bills of exchange, are generally accepted (with safeguards) in
the business world.

Legal tender is generally defined as:

    That which is acceptable in a court of law in
    settlement of a debt, ie, any bank notes; bronze
    coin to the value of 20p; nickel coin to the value
    of £5; 50p coins to the value of £10 and £1 coins
    to any value.

A cheque is generally defined as:

    An unconditional order in writing, addressed by an
    account holder to the manager of a named bank,
    ordering him to pay a certain sum of money, written
    in words and figures from the named account to a
    third party. The order has to be dated and it has
    to be signed by the person making the order.

A Bill of Exchange is generally defined as:

    An unconditional order in writing, addressed by one
    person to another, signed by the person giving it,
    requiring the person to whom it is addressed to pay
    on demand, or at a fixed determinable future time,
    a certain sum of money, to, or to the order of, a
    specified person or to the bearer.

12

Exercise 5

Practise shoulder headings – see page 6. Use single line spacing. **Margins**: left 38 mm (1½ in); right 25 mm (1 in). (See page 36).

<u>GARDEN FLOWERS</u>

<u>Types</u>

Garden flowers should not be confused with greenhouse varieties, many of which cannot withstand temperatures below 20 ^{o}C (68 ^{o}F) for long periods of time. There are 3 types: annuals, biennials and perennials.

ANNUALS

These flowers complete their life cycle, seed to seed, in one year and there are 2 kinds generally grown. <u>Half hardy annuals</u> need a longer growing season to reach maturity than <u>hardy annuals</u> – a group of flowers which can survive the winter if they are sown outside in the autumn. Half hardy annuals are started in the greenhouse or on the windowsill of the living room where the warmth encourages easy germination. This group of flowers should be planted out at the end of May when all danger of late frost has passed. Hardy annuals can be sown outside in the spring (March to May) or the autumn (August to September) where they are to flower.

BIENNIALS

This group of flowers requires 2 growing seasons from planting to seed production – after which they die. Most of the spring flowers fall into this category and the seeds should be sown in May or June in prepared beds outside ready for planting in their permanent position in the autumn.

PERENNIALS

These flowers come year after year and can be grown from seed or from the division of old plants once their flowering season has finished. Seed is usually set in May or June for flowering plants the following year – after which stocks may be increased as previously indicated. Most of these flowers need cutting back to ground level after flowering.

Exercise 6
Practise shoulder headings – see page 6. Use single line spacing. **Margins**; left 38 mm (1½ in); right 25 mm (1 in). (See page 36.)

THE HEDGE

A vanishing feature of the English countryside

"Hedge. A fence of bushes, low trees, turf or stone forming a barrier." A typical description of part of the English scene which is rapidly vanishing as farmers seek to enlarge fields in the interests of mechanisation and profits. From this movement die 2 other traditional arts – hedge trimming and, more importantly in many eyes, hedge-laying.

HEDGE TRIMMING

Living hedges need sympathetic handling if they are to thrive and the process of hedge trimming is an attempt to keep them tidy. The problem with living hedges is that it is always the new growth which is cut in the trimming process and after a time the main growths die back or the base of the hedge becomes thin and animals can push through. The original values of hedges were to mark boundaries and to keep in a range of animals – sheep and cattle in particular. Modern hedge trimming is nothing short of butchery to many eyes as the machinery flays the living bushes/trees but farmers can point to the expense of labour when traditional tools are employed.

HEDGE-LAYING

Laying a hedge is the creation of a stock-proof barrier which will, with intermediate trimming, last for up to 20 years before it has to be relaid. The hedge is first cleaned using hooks or slashers (the style of which varies from county to county). Pleachers, strong growths which form the foundation of the hedge, are then prepared and cut at an angle near the base. A strip of bark must be left or the growth will die. The pleachers are then woven between a line of stakes hammered into the line of the hedge and tied into position until new horizontal growth can fill up the gaps. A well laid hedge is good enough to deter the most escape-minded sheep.

14

Exercise 7

Practise paragraph headings – see page 6. Use single line spacing. **Margins**: left 38 mm ($1\frac{1}{2}$ in); right 25 mm (1 in). (See page 36.)

CLASSICAL MUSIC

Its early masters

To many ears, the best of what members of European culture call 'classical music' was written before the middle of the last century. Whilst some people would claim that the last of the classical school (Richard Strauss?) died this century others think that the period ended with Brahms (1833-97).

Bach (1685-1750) is considered to be the first great classical composer by many experts. His output was vast and his best works are often thought to be his instrumental works and his orchestral suites. His solo violin works are outstanding.

Handel (1685-1759) unlike Bach (who wrote to please his employers) wrote for the wider public and because of this he was more widely recognised in his life-time. His greatest works were almost certainly his oratorios although during his life-time he was probably better known for his operas.

Haydn (1732-1809), affectionately known as 'Papa Haydn', was certainly the father of the symphony (he wrote over a hundred) and the string quartet. Although he wrote a great variety of music he was not noted for his concertos. He certainly paved the way for Beethoven's symphonic works.

Mozart (1756-1791) is arguably the greatest writer of piano concertos who has ever lived and many consider his symphonies to be the equal of Haydn's. But for his early death he would have almost certainly added a new dimension to the classical repertoire.

Beethoven (1770-1827) was the first composer to earn his living from his writing and his greatest contributions were to build on the symphonic foundations of Haydn in the development of the symphony and those of Mozart in the development of the piano concerto. Compare his "Eroica" symphony with any of Haydn's or his "Emperor" concerto with any of Mozart's to see the development he effected.

Exercise 8
Practise paragraph headings – see page 6. Use single line spacing. **Margins**: left 38 mm (1½ in); right 25 mm (1 in). (See page 36.)

TELEPHONE CALL SERVICES

ADC calls (short for Advice of Duration and Charge) are used when the user wants to know the cost of the call just made. ADC calls have to be made via the operator who monitors how long the call takes and then advises how much it has cost.

Freefone calls enable clients of firms to telephone the firm without paying. The user dials the operator and says which Freefone number is required – before being connected free of charge. The receiver of the call pays for it.

Reversed charge calls should not be confused with Freefone calls. To reverse the charges the user has first to dial the operator who then asks if the person the user wishes to contact will accept the call – and thus pay for it. If the person at that number not is prepared to accept the call, the call cannot be made.

Fixed time calls are calls which the operator undertakes to connect within a limited time (usually 10 minutes). These calls can be booked in advance and the service enables users to have a clear idea of when they can contact required numbers.

Personal calls are those made to a particular person and they are made through the operator who will dial a number until the person required is available. As soon as they are the operator informs the person wanting to make the call.

Telephone credit cards enable telephone users to dial from public telephones without ready money. The user dials the operator, indicates the number of the credit card and is then connected – the charge being made to the credit card holder later. Each card is issued against a quarterly fee and calls are charged at the normal rates applying.

16

Exercise 9
Practise side (marginal) headings – see page 6. Use single line spacing.
Margins: left 38 mm (1½ in); right 25 mm (1 in). Leave 3 spaces between
the longest heading (TRAIL BLAZER) and the paragraphs.

F A S H I O N   S H O E S

The David Anthony collection

These shoes are available only by mail order and are invoiced
at our current prices. We undertake to hold prices for a
period of 12 months from 1 January each year and to exchange
or refund for your absolute satisfaction.

EASIWEARER   Combining lightness with the durability that
              only quality leather and expert workmanship can
              bring. Tough enough to withstand the most
              testing of outdoor conditions yet stylish
              enough to be worn as a house shoe.

              Sizes: Women 3-9; Men 6-12. Rich tan or cream.

TRAIL BLAZER Casual wear which is real value for money. Our
              own design which ensures maximum comfort. Of
              sturdy construction, the design incorporates
              special hand stitching for extra strength and
              fashionable adjustable leather straps.

              Sizes: Women 3-9; Men 3-12. Teak or ebony.

EXCURSION   The ultimate in lightweight casual wear. Made
              from specially selected leather and designed to
              our own inimitable standards for practical town
              or country wear. Extra strong heels and soles
              for the most discriminating wearer.

              Sizes: Women 3-10; Men 5-12. Oak or cream.

ACTIVITY   An expertly designed boot made from supple
              leather uppers and a durable heel and sole
              unit.

              Sizes: Women 3-10; Men 3-12. Tan or charcoal.

Exercise 10
Practise side (marginal) headings – see page 6. Use single line spacing.
Margins: left 38 mm (1½ in); right 25 mm (1 in). (See page 36.)

MOTORWAY PESTS

Speaking about the standard of driving on motorways a spokesman of one of the leading motoring clubs called attention to three species of 'pests' or drivers who created problems for others. No doubt they are familiar to all motorway users!

The lane crawler	This driver is the one who drives in the middle lane of three-lane motorways, usually at a speed some way below the legal limit. Even when the inside lane is totally clear this driver keeps to the centre lane so that anyone wishing to overtake must either break the law and drive up the inside lane or take the (often crowded) outside lane. Lorry drivers especially loathe this pest because they are not supposed to use the outside lane of three.
The winker	Divine right permits this driver to give the briefest flash on the indicators before moving from slip roads to join the motorway or to move from the outside lane, across the two inside lanes to leave the motorway. The same logic dictates that this driver also changes lanes at the very last moment – no matter who is coming up behind.
The outside laner	This driver sees the outside lane as a personal racing track and blasts up it at speeds far in excess of the legal limit. Those who are unfortunate to be (legally) overtaking in this lane are blasted out of the way by flashing lights or blaring horns.

Part of the problem stems from the fact that the driving test does not include motorway driving. Any driver passing a test in some quiet rural country town is permitted to drive on any public road, irrespective of their experience or knowledge of driving at speed in heavy traffic.

18 ·

Exercise 11

Practise numbered paragraphs – see page 7. These Roman numerals are
bracketed on both sides and are outside the paragraphs. **Margins:** any
suitable width. To set the tab for the paragraphs when using a typewriter,
tap from the left margin the longest number, e.g. (viii) and 2 or 3 spaces.
If you are using a word processor, follow the manual's instructions.

EVERSURE INSURANCE

Guaranteed plan for life insurance

(i)   No sales staff will call on you. Simply complete the
        application form and post it to us.

(ii)   You will have full cover from the day your form of
        application is accepted by us.

(iii)   Provided you answer our questions satisfactorily you
        will not be asked to undergo a medical examination.

(iv)   After a period of 3 years your policy will acquire a
        cash-in and loan value.

(v)   The monthly premiums shown on your policy will remain
        the same - there will be no increases.

(vi)   Provided you pay the premiums we will not be able to
        cancel your policy.

(vii)   Your benefits are fixed at the time of the acceptance
        of your policy and they cannot be decreased by us.

(viii) You have 10 days to examine the policy and during
        that time you can select which of the monthly
        premiums you wish to pay.

(ix)   All premiums are eligible for tax relief.

(x)   Benefits will be free of income tax and capital gains
        tax (under the law as it currently stands).

IF YOU COMPLETE YOUR APPLICATION FORM AND RETURN IT TO US
WITHIN 28 DAYS WE WILL WAIVE YOUR FIRST MONTH'S PREMIUM. THE
OFFER APPLIES TO BOTH UK AND NON-UK RESIDENTS.

Exercise 12
Practise blocked paragraphs in double line spacing – see page 3. **Margins**:
any suitable width.

LIBRARY RULES

1   No material may be removed without first filling in the

    appropriate return slip.

2   All books must be returned within the month allowed or

    they must be renewed. Books requested by another reader

    cannot be renewed.

3   All books must be returned to the library before the end

    of the summer term.

4   A maximum of five books are allowed in one person's

    possession at any time.

5   Material borrowed from the library must be kept in good

    condition – otherwise a charge may be made to replace it.

6   Books in stock may be reserved. Library staff are always

    pleased to hear suggestions for the ordering of books.

7   Reference books must not be removed from the library.

    They may be used in the reading room of the reference

    section under the supervision of the library staff.

20

Exercise 13

Practise indented paragraphs produced in double line spacing – see page 3.
Margins: any suitable width. Note the use of shoulder headings.

STUDENTS' GUILD

OBJECTS

    a) To encourage and foster corporate spirit among all the students of the College by providing the means for social and cultural activities.

    b) To provide a focal point for the expression of opinion among the student body and to receive suggestions from students relating to all aspects of the social and domestic life of the College.

    c) To provide the opportunity for social contact between the students and the Teaching and Administrative Staff.

    d) To provide the means of representing the body of College students in external contacts involving the College such as sporting, cultural and academic matters.

MEMBERSHIP

    Membership is automatically conferred on all staff at the time of their appointment and on all students at the time of their enrolment. On leaving College staff and students may continue membership on payment of a fee agreed annually.

Exercise 14
Practise blocked paragraphs produced in double line spacing – see page 3.
Margins: any suitable width.

GUARANTEE

We, THERMALECTRIC, guarantee that should our heating product prove to be defective by reason of faulty workmanship or material within 12 months of the date of purchase we will replace it free of charge on condition that:-

(1)   The appliance has been correctly installed and used only on the supply circuit or voltage stamped on the rating plate.

(2)   The appliance has been used in accordance with the operating and installation instructions and that it has not been subject to mis-use, neglect, or tampering.

(3)   The appliance has not been taken apart or repaired by any person other than authorised by us.

(4)   Evidence of the date of purchase is included with any claim. Such evidence must be in the form of an invoice, receipt or a hire purchase document.

(5)   Claims are forwarded direct to our registered office or to the dealer/agent supplying the appliance. Claims to our registered office should be made in writing.

Exercise 15

Practise hanging paragraphs produced in double line spacing – see page 4.
Margins: any suitable width.

PARTICULARS OF HOUSES

The following particulars apply to all houses built on the

Oaklands Development – both Phases I and II.

1   The walls are to be of cavity construction with facing

     bricks externally except where 'Tyrolean' rendering,

     timber boarding, vertical tiling or art stone relief

     panels are shown by the Architect.

2   All pitched roofs are to be covered with best quality

     concrete tiles laid on battens over a layer of felt.

3   All flat roofs (used on garages only) are to be covered

     with mineral surfaced felt with an asbestos underlayer

     laid on boards and joists.

4   Ground floors will be of solid construction throughout

     with a polythene membrane. They will be covered with

     best quality thermoplastic tiles – option of colours.

5   The first floors will be pine boards laid over timber

     joists for all rooms except bathrooms where the

     flooring material is negotiable.

6   Ducted warm air gas fired central heating will be

     provided throughout with vents in all rooms.

Exercise 16
Practise insetting - see page 5. Use single line spacing and inset the left
margin only. **Margins**: any suitable width.

TAXATION

PURPOSE

The purposes of taxation are to raise revenue from which
the Government can make public expenditure and to regulate the
economy. The effect of taxing products is to make them more
expensive to the consumer and thus to lessen demand - and
there are times when Governments want to dampen down the
volume of sales. An example of this is the tax on cigarettes.

Smoking is considered to be damaging to health and it is
generally considered that the more expensive Governments
make smoking products the less will be purchased. This
lessens demands made on medical resources by smoking-
related complaints. A similar logic is applied to the
taxes on all forms of alcohol - spirits in particular.

KINDS

There are several forms of taxation used by Governments.
These tend to fall into 2 basic kinds; direct and indirect.

Direct taxes are those which individuals and firms pay
directly out of income. Self-employed individuals pay their
tax like firms - on an annual assessment. People employed by
others pay their tax as it falls due on a Pay As You Earn
(PAYE) basis.

Each individual is given certain tax free allowances
which when added together form the basis of a code
number. This code number indicates to employers how
much tax free pay each individual employee is entitled
to - and how much tax should be deducted from the wages
or salary to be paid.

Indirect taxes are taxes which are included in the
purchase price of goods and services. Many countries have
some form of sales tax. Examples of indirect taxes are VAT,
(Value Added Tax) and Customs and Excise Duties.

24

Decimal notation

Whole numbers and decimals are often used to indicate sections and subsections of work in addition to Roman numerals and bracketed and unbracketed letters. In some cases all numbers are followed by a decimal point, e.g. 1.2.1., while in others the final decimal point is omitted. Leave 2 or 3 spaces, consistently, between the decimal notation and the material to which it refers.

Exercise 17

Type the exercise on a sheet of A4 paper using decimal notation.

GENERAL TERMS AND CONDITIONS OF EMPLOYMENT - CONTINUED

10 MOVEMENT WITHIN DEPARTMENTS

   10.1 The Company may move employees from job to job or Department to Department in order to save an employee from short time working or redundancy.

   10.2 The employee in question has the right to refuse such a move if he/she has good reason for doing so but since such a move would be requested in order to avoid 10.1 above and, if necessary, he/she will be given training and subsidy in the new job the consent must not be unreasonably refused.

   10.3 In the event of a disagreement as to 10.2 the matter will be, in the first instance, referred to the Employer/Employee Working Party for consideration. The employee may make a personal statement to the Working Party or may be represented by a union official.

   10.4 In the event of 10.3 failing the matter shall be referred to the usual outside agencies whose findings shall be binding on both sides.

11 EMPLOYEE'S NOTICE

   11.1 An employee may terminate employment during the first 12 months of employment by giving one week's notice.

Exercise 18
Type the exercise on a suitable sheet of paper using decimal notation.

COLPRO (1979) PLC

EMPLOYER/EMPLOYEE WORKING PARTY – TERMS OF REFERENCE

1   MEMBERSHIP

    1.1   The Working Party shall consist of 5 members from each side.

    1.2   Worker representatives shall be elected annually by the whole work force by secret ballot held the first Monday in May.

    1.3   Any employee who has been in the continuous service of the Company for a period of 2 years shall be eligible for election.

    1.4   Employer representatives shall be nominated by the Board of Directors but they must be in the employment of the Company as full-time directors or be shareholders holding not less than 1000 shares.

2   DEPUTIES

    2.1   Worker representatives who are unable to attend any meeting shall be allowed to send a deputy.

    2.2   Deputies shall be the next 5 persons receiving votes in the annual ballot.

    2.3   Employer deputies shall be nominated by the Board.

3   MEETINGS

    3.1   Meetings of the Working Party shall be held monthly.

    3.2   Minutes shall be produced and circulated prior to each meeting and representatives shall receive a copy of the agenda not less than 5 working days prior to each meeting.

CHAPTER 3

FORMS OF ADDRESS

When typing the names of individuals, partnerships or companies and addresses *standard* or *open punctuation* may be used (the same applies to degrees, qualifications, titles and decorations, etc.). The modern practice is to use open punctuation and so the first part of this section concentrates on this.

3.1 OPEN PUNCTUATION

Initials and qualifications
There are several styles in use but the one adopted in this text is universally acceptable. When typing the initials of a person or company, etc. leave one space between each initial, e.g. R A Heath, J G & J C Ltd, J Turner plc. When typing degrees or qualifications type them after the name of the individual with no space between the letters of the degree or qualification but with one space between groups or letters, e.g. M A Hewines BA FRSA FSCT.

Forms of address
Always use a courtesy title when addressing individuals:

Mr (for *Mister*) when addressing a male, typed before his initials, first names, or surname only (if neither initial(s) nor first name(s) are known), e.g. Mr W R Yates, Mr David Evans, Mr Simpkiss.

Esq (for *Esquire*) may be typed after a male's name instead of typing Mr before it, e.g. W R Yates Esq, David Evans Esq.

Rev (for *Reverend*) and *Dr* (*Doctor*) replace Mr, e.g. Rev A W Roberts, Dr P J Davies.

Messrs (for *Messieurs*) when addressing more than one male, e.g. Messrs Roberts & Davis.

Miss when addressing a single lady, e.g. Miss M A Hewines, Miss Susan Old.

Mrs (for *Mistress*) when addressing a married women, e.g. Mrs C N Wilson, Mrs David Hartley.

The Misses when addressing more than one single lady of the same name, e.g The Misses Jenkinson.

Ms is used by some women or when addressing a woman whose status is not known, e.g. Ms J A Turner, Ms Roberts.

Mesdames is used when addressing more than one married woman of the same name, e.g. Mesdames Patterson.

When addressing limited companies use *Ltd* for private limited companies, *PLC* (*plc*) for public limited companies and *Co* for unlimited companies. Do not use a courtesy title even if the name of the company includes the name of an individual, e.g. David Jenkins Ltd, John Spencer plc, Paula Evans & Co.

When addressing organisations do not use a courtsey title, e.g. Bristol Sports & Social Club.

Use of the ampersand
The ampersand (&) takes the place of the word 'and' when typing:

the names of companies, e.g. Jenkins & Roberts Co, Walters & Wright Ltd, Andrews & Marks plc;

the names of partnerships, e.g. Messrs Symmonds, Turner & Vickers;

the names of couples, e.g. Mr & Mrs C A Brockwell;

numbers in addresses, e.g. 7 & 8 Weston Street;

certain standard abbreviations, e.g. R & D Department.

Letters after names
Letters representing decorations, qualifications, etc. should be typed after the name of individual in the order:

military decorations, e.g. DSO;
civil decorations, e.g. MBE;
university degrees, e.g. BSc;
member of Parliament (MP);
legal post (JP).

The words Sen (Senior) and Jun (Junior) are sometimes used to distinguish father and son and they are typed after the name of the individual in the position of Esq, e.g. John Walters Sen, John Walters Jun. If the name of the individual is a professor the word is typed before the name, e.g. Professor W A Taylor or Prof W A Taylor.

Foreign equivalents
When addressing individuals in a foreign country the foreign equivalents of English language titles should be used but if there is any doubt use the English forms of address outlined earlier.

3.2 ADDRESSING ENVELOPES

Envelopes should be addressed in accordance with the current Post Office regulations. The correct order for an address in the UK is as follows:

1. The name of the addressee (see previous pages for the use of courtesy titles and letters after names).
2. The number of the house or the name of the house if it does not have a number and the name of the road, street, avenue, etc.
3. The name of the locality where required by the Post Office.
4. The name of the hamlet or village – in a country district.
5. The name of the postal town (which might not be the same as the actual town) typed in *capital letters*. If the addressee considers that his address has little connection with the postal town the word 'via' may be typed before the postal town.
6. The name of the county – where required.
7. The postcode, shown as the last item in the address, typed on a line by itself, in 2 parts separated by 1 or 2 spaces, *unpunctuated* and typed in *capital letters*.

The correct order for an overseas address is as follows:

1. The name of the addressee.
2. The number of the house or, if the house does not have a number, its name. If the address is a flat or a suite of offices the number of the flat or the floor on which it is situated should be given together with the name or number of the block of which the premises are part.
3. The name of the road, street, etc. If the address is a flat or a suite of offices, the number of the flat or the floor on which it is situated should be given together with the name or number of the block to which the premises are part.
4. The name of the place – typed in *capital letters*. If there is no Post Office you should give the name of the nearest Post Office.
5. The initials or number of the postal district.

6. The name of the province, state department and postal address code where appropriate.

7. The name of the country, typed in *capital letters*.

For specific details of overseas addresses, however, you should consult the relevant page of *The Post Office Guide.*

Position of the address

Envelopes should be addressed in the lower part towards the right-hand side of the front. Special instructions concerned with the address (For the attention of [see also page 51], Private, Confidential, etc.) should be typed all in capital letters or with initial capitals and underscore one blank line (turn up 2 single lines) above the address or to the left of the address (but not below it). Special instructions concerning the delivery service (e.g. Poste Restante or Freepost) should be typed after the name of the addressee. Special instructions for the Post Office (Airmail, Par Avion, Registered Delivery, Recorded Delivery, etc.) should be typed in the top left-hand corner.

Addresses should be typed in single line spacing unless the envelope is a large one and the address is a short one – in which case single, line-and-a-half or double line spacing may be used. If an address has to be shortened because of addressing machine – or word processor – limitations, the postal town and county may be typed on the same line and if need be (because of the same limitations) the postcode may be typed as the last item of the address, typed on the same line as the postal town or county, separated from it by at least 2 and preferably 6 spaces.

Other mail

Parcels should follow the same rules as envelopes except that the address may be typed on a label and stuck on to the parcel.

The name and address of the sender should be typed on the back of envelopes or be stuck on parcels in case of non-delivery.

Postcards should follow the rules previously outlined. See also page 167.

Typing names and addresses on envelopes
To address envelopes:

1. Set a left margin so that the longest line in the address starts roughly in the centre of the width of the envelope.

2. Turn up sufficient spaces so that the first line of the address (or the instructions which precede it) are typed in the lower part of the depth of the envelope.

3. Type each line of the address from the left margin so that when typed it is justified on the left, e.g.

```
Miss B S Matthews BA       Dr G W Sleath
The Willows               9803 75 Avenue
45 Earl Street            EDMONTON
CORBY                     Alberta
Northants                 CANADA
NN17 1NN                  T6E 1H9
```

The position of each address will depend on the size of the envelope being used and the length of the address. See page 31 for envelope sizes.

The style of punctuation used on the envelope should follow that used when producing the letter – see pages 43 to 85.

Addressing labels

Labels to be stuck on parcels and packets should be addressed according to the Post Office regulations and with a straight (justified) margin, as above.

3.3 STANDARD PUNCTUATION

The courtesy title should be followed by a full stop when abbreviated, e.g. Mr.; Mrs.; Rev.; Dr.; Esq.; Sen.; etc. When the courtesy title preceeds the name or initial(s) it should be followed by a space, e.g. Mr. Peter Smith, Mrs. J. Yates. When the courtesy title follows the name a comma should be typed immediately after the name and a space left between the comma and the courtesy title, e.g. John Andrew, Esq.

Initials in the name should be followed by a full stop and a space should be left after each full stop and what follows, e.g. T. A. Smith.

Letters after the name should be followed by a full stop with no space between the full stops and what follows except that the final full stop in a group should be followed by a comma and a space left between it and the next group, e.g.

```
Mr. Y. P. Gough, B.A., B.Sc.
```

When addressing envelopes using standard punctuation, each line of the address should end with a comma except the last item before the postcode which should be followed by a full stop. The postcode must *never* be punctuated, e.g.

```
Messrs. Walters, Roberts & Turner,    Mr. & Mrs. D. N. Oldfield,
Unit 5,                               78 Church Lane,
Manchester Road,                      HORSHAM,
LIVERPOOL.                            West Sussex.
L70 2TT                               RH12 1ZA
```

3.4 COUNTY NAMES

With the following exceptions, all county names should be typed in full to avoid confusion. They may be typed standard or open punctuation following the style of the rest of the address.

Beds	Bedfordshire	N Yorkshire	North Yorkshire
Berks	Berkshire	Northants	Northamptonshire
Bucks	Buckinghamshire	Northd	Northumberland
Cambs	Cambridgeshire	Notts	Nottinghamshire
Co Derry	Co Londonderry	Oxon	Oxfordshire
Co Durham	County Durham	S Glam	South Glamorgan
E Sussex	East Sussex	S Humberside	South Humberside
Glos	Gloucestershire	S Yorkshire	South Yorkshire
Hants	Hampshire	Staffs	Staffordshire
Herts	Hertfordshire	Tyne & Wear	Tyne and Wear
Lancs	Lancashire	W Glam	West Glamorgan
Leics	Leicestershire	W Midlands	West Midlands
Lincs	Lincolnshire	W Sussex	West Sussex
M Glam	Mid Glamorgan	W Yorkshire	West Yorkshire
Middx	Middlesex	Wilts	Wiltshire
N Humberside	North Humberside	Worcs	Worcestershire

3.5 ADDRESSING MATERIAL TO THE UK FROM OVERSEAS

The same rules apply as for internal addresses except that the country should be typed in *capital letters* before the line on which the postcode is typed, e.g.

```
Mrs V A Matthews        Mr J V Hughes
34 Lichfield Road       89 Thames Valley Lane
FELTHAM                 FISHGUARD
Middx                   Dyfed
ENGLAND                 WALES
TW14 OTG                SA65 9RH
```

The above examples are open punctuation – standard punctuation may be used. See the pages which follow for envelope addressing exercises.

3.6 ENVELOPE SIZES

Metric envelopes, the C range, are designed to be used with A size paper – see Appendix B. The most commonly used C sized envelopes are as follows:

Designation	Size (mm)	Uses
C3	324 × 458	Takes A3 paper flat
C4	229 × 324	Takes A4 paper flat
C5	162 × 229	Takes A5 paper flat *or* A4 paper folded once
C6	114 × 162	Takes A6 paper flat *or* A5 paper folded once *or* A4 folded twice
C5/6 (DL)	110 × 220	Takes A4 paper folded twice into three *or* A5 folded once *or* 2/3 A4 folded once

British Standard envelopes are sometimes used as follows:

Designation	Size (mm)	Uses
B4	250 × 353	Legal documents, company reports and accounts, calendars, examination papers
B5	176 × 250	Reply envelopes, catalogues, brochures, half foolscap material
B6	125 × 176	General commercial correspondence, computer punch cards, dividend warrants, greetings cards

Care must be taken to ensure that metric sizes of paper are used with metric sizes of envelopes and that metric and imperial paper and envelopes are not mixed.

Exercise 19
Practise envelope addressing – see pages 28–31.
Fold sheets of paper to represent envelopes of varying sizes and address them with the following information, making any corrections required.

1   Mrs Betty Hollingsworth, 42 Highfields Road, BURNLEY, Lancs. BB10 1UZ

2   Henry Tenens Engineering (Andover) Ltd, The Clock House, 142 Coney Street, ANDOVER, Hants. SP10 3SA

3   Mr J W Turner BA FSCT, Flat 34, Bristol Towers, Highgate Road, LONDON. NW5 1RS

4   FOR THE ATTENTION OF MISS F HICKMAN, J & S Motors Ltd, 8 London Road, Medway, ROCHESTER, Kent. ME99 1AA

5   PRIVATE AND CONFIDENTIAL, Mrs Ian Weston, 3 Telford Lane, STOCKPORT, Cheshire. SK1 1GW

6   Jack Cotton & Partners, Chartered Surveyors, Valuers, Estate Agents and Auctioneers, 9 Whitburn Street, Bamber Bridge, PRESTON. PR5 8AX

7   The Misses Walker, Oakdene, John Bright Avenue, TENBY, West Wales. SA70 8AP

8   Harry Feltham Senior, 9 The Parade, BOURNEMOUTH. BH8 8XH

9   Lane Percy Group plc, Unit 10, Webner Industrial Estate, Albion Road, LEIGH, Lancs. WN7 1BR

10   Dr W A Elwell, The Surgery, 9a Haynes Lane, WEMBLEY, Middlesex. HA0 1BR

11   Sir John Marks QC, The House, Shaftesbury Lane, CHELTENHAM, Glos. GL52 5EP

12   Major Andrew Summerfield-Vernon MC DSO, 154 Essex Lane, LEICESTER. LE1 4SG

Exercise 20
Practise addressing envelopes – see pages 28-31.
Fold sheets of paper to represent envelopes of varying sizes and address
them with the following, making any corrections required.

1   Miss Wendy Lloyd, Grand Hotel, Dam 9, Amsterdam 1012 JS,
    Netherlands.

2   Christiani & Nielsen A/S, DK-1501, Copenhagen V, Vester
    Farimagsgade 41, Denmark.

3   ATTENTION: Dr V Y Giuliano, Maschinenfabrika Heid Ag,
    1015 Vienna 1, Mahlerstr 6, Austria.

4   Mr & Mrs A M Glaze, c/o Southern Cross Hotel, 104
    Bathurst Street, Sydney, Australia.

5   F A B Ltd, 18-19 Shimon Hatzadek Street, PO Box 8155,
    Tel Aviv, Israel.

6   Townsend & Mears Inc, PO Box 3, Clinton Drive, Houston,
    Texas 77001, USA.

7   Orbitsports Ltd, Pate Road, Box 14075, Nairobi, Kenya.

8   Mrs R Bobzom, 4 Anguwan Rimi Road, Kaduna, Nigeria.

9   Rev W T Akamiokhor, 90 Cuffe Parade, Colaba, Bombay,
    India.

10 PAR AVION, Andrew Black Jun, High House, 4 Aberdeen Road,
    Glenrothes, Fife, Scotland. KY7 4NX

11 Concor Construction (Pty) Ltd, Johannesburg 2001, Concor
    House, 13 Church Street, South Africa.

12 Mme M S La Trobe, 75781 Paris Cedex 6, 37 BD Montmorency,
    France.

13 From Spain to: Ms Alice Hartill, 8a The Green, Rugby,
    Warwickshire, England. CV21 3AP

14 Mr Paul Niedzewtzki MD, 1 Kolokotroni Square, Athens,
    Greece.

THE PLACEMENT OF
MATERIAL ON THE PAGE

Apart from the need to be accurate, typists need to be able to place material on the page satisfactorily and this means paying attention to top and bottom margins as well as those on either side of the page. Good placement of any printed or typed material adds to its impact. This section is concerned with the placement of general material and letters (see pages 86–142 for the placement of displays and tabulations). The latter part of this section offers some advice to users of word processors.

4.1 GENERAL MATERIAL

To enable you to produce satisfactory margins at the top and bottom and on each side of a page when using a typewriter you should first calculate the number of typing words in the material. Those using a word processor or microcomputer with a word processing program will know that the placement of much material is automatic and the handbook will tell you what commands to feed into your machine to set margins - it varies from machine to machine and program to program.

A typing word is generally taken to consist of 5 letters or spaces. It is usual to leave a minimum *top margin* of 25 mm (1 in) and a minimum *bottom margin* of 30 mm (1¼ in) on both A5 and A4 sheets of paper (the sizes most commonly used in typewriting). The most commonly used size used with word processors is A4 using a single sheet feed, though most machines use continuous stationery. It is usual to leave a minimum *left margin* of 25 mm (1 in) and a minimum *right margin* of 13 mm (½ in) on A4 sheets of paper and minimum left and right margins of 13 mm (½ in) when using A5 sheets.

It is not possible to be totally accurate when describing what margins to use with what length of material because of such factors as style of presentation (blocked or indented), the amount of displayed material within general material and the line spacing being used. The margins given below should be taken as an indication of the margins to be used and as a guide to the satisfactory placement of material on the page.

Margins to be used on A4 paper

12 pitch (elite)

Words	Spacing	Margins
380–400	double	18–88
750–780	single	18–88
435–450	double	12–94
870–900	single	12–94

10 pitch (pica)

Words	Spacing	Margins
300–330	double	15–72
620–650	single	15–72
380–400	double	10–77
650–700	single	10–77

Material of under 300 words pica or 380 word elite should be produced on A5 paper with a minimum left margin of 25 mm (1 in) and a minimum right margin of 13 mm ($\frac{1}{2}$ in) when using a typewriter - it may not be practical to use A5 paper with some word processors.

15 pitch

Words	Spacing	Margins
460–480	double	23–110
950–970	single	23–110
530–550	double	15–110
1070–1090	single	15–110

Material of under 500 words should be produced on A5 paper with a minimum left margin of 25 mm (1 in) and a minimum right margin of 13 mm ($\frac{1}{2}$ in) using single line spacing.

Equal margins are acceptable. If one margin has to be wider than the other, the left margin should always be wider than the right - to allow for stitching if the work is to be bound, or for filing purposes.

Lines of type down a page

Most typewriters produce 6 lines of type of each 25 mm (1 in), though some machines produce various combinations up to 8 lines to each 25 mm. When using a typewriter or printer producing 6 lines to each 25 mm there are 57 usable lines of type (after making due allowances for top and bottom margins) on a sheet of A4 paper (210 × 297 mm) when using single line spacing and producing general material. There are 29 usable lines when using A4 paper and double line spacing. When using A5 paper (148 × 210 mm) there are 36 usable single lines available, and 18 usable lines when using double line spacing. When using a typewriter or printer with 8 lines to each 25 mm there are 76 usable lines using A4 paper

(210 x 297 mm) and single line spacing, 38 usable lines when using double line spacing; 48 usable lines when using A5 paper and single line spacing (148 x 210 mm) and 24 usable lines when using double line spacing.

Letters

Exact instructions concerning placement are impossible because of such factors as the style of the letter (blocked or semi-blocked), the amount of display within the letter and the number of headings. The following applies when single line spacing is being used.

In elite type (12 pitch)

Words	Paper	Margins
under 150	A5	12-64
150-200	A4	24-76
250-300	A4	18-88
350-400	A4	12-88

Longer letters require a continuation sheet

In pica type (10 pitch)

Words	Paper	Margins
under 120	A5	not less than 10-53
120-250	A4	15-53
250-350	A4	10-72

Longer letters require a continuation sheet

15 pitch

Words	Paper	Margins
under 275	A5	15-80
275-700	A4	23-110
700-800	A4	15-110
800-850	A4	15-115

Longer letters require a continuation sheet

4.2 MEMORY TYPEWRITERS, WORD PROCESSORS AND MICROCOMPUTERS

Memory typewriter, word processor and microcomputer memories are measured in terms of bytes. A byte is a single unit - 5 bytes make a standard typing word. For convenience it is now common practice to talk in terms of kilobytes (Kbytes) or K for short. A kilobyte is 1024 bytes or 204.5 standard typing words. A memory of 12K holds 12 x 1024 bytes = 12 288 separate units of information or 2458 standard typing words. Most word processors and microcomputers use some form of *floppy disk* for ROM memory (Read Only Memory) and the amount of storage capacity depends on the machine being used and the type of disk. Some disks are single sided and single density while others are double sided and double density. The kind of disk usable with each machine is determined by the disk drives. Before storing information on any disk it has to be formatted -

made into files. It follows that the amount of storage space on any disk is determined by two factors – the overall size of the disk and its density and the number of files it holds. If you are using a word processor or micro-computer you may find that you have available storage capacity on a disk but that you have run out of available files – in other words, you have a lot of files which are less than full of information.

As a general guide you should reckon that a sheet of A4 paper set in 10 pitch (pica type) holds 2K of information while the same sheet set in 12 pitch (elite type) holds 3K of information. An A4 sheet set in 15 pitch holds up to 4K. Average letters occupy 2K, though, obviously, longer letters can occupy much more.

4.3 THE CORRECTION OF ERRORS

All typists and microcomputer users make errors from time to time and these have to be corrected. Good typing technique and practice will help to prevent most errors but if they are made and you need to correct them there are several alternatives. The method you use will, in part, be deter-mined by the machine you are using.

Manual typewriters

If you are using a manual machine you have 2 alternatives. You can either remove the error using a typing eraser or you can cover it up using correct-ing paper or fluid.

To correct an error using an eraser you should first choose a suitable eraser. A good typing eraser is one which contains abrasive material which will remove the ink from the page. A soft india-rubber or pencil rubber is not satisfactory. Perhaps the most convenient typing eraser is the one made by Blaisdell which comes in the form of a 'self-sharpening' cardboard pencil – though there are several other satisfactory makes of eraser available. When you discover that you have made a mistake, move the carriage as far as possible to one side or the other using the margin release key – this will save erasure dust from dropping into your machine as you make the correction. Wind the paper on to the erasure platform above the roller or platen and gently but firmly remove the error – taking care not to rub a hole in the paper. Smooth down the correction using the wrong end of a pen or some other tool and return to the printing point. Type in the correction with the same amount of pressure used for your normal typing.

To correct an error using correcting paper you should first obtain paper the same colour as the paper you are typing on. When you find that you have made an error, back-space to the point of the error, insert a sheet of correcting paper between the type face and the error and type the error again. This will cause some of the substance on the back of the correcting paper to cover your error. Back-space once more and type in the required correction.

To correct an error using correcting fluid you should first obtain correcting fluid which is the same colour as the paper you are using. When you discover that you have made an error simply use the brush with the fluid to paint over the error and when the fluid has dried completely type over the required correction. Always keep your fluid thinned down so that it is not obvious when used – and take care to not let it get dirty through too much use.

Correcting paper and correcting fluid can be used with any kind of typewriter – as indeed can a typing eraser. The problem with the latter is that it can cause a lot of dust if not correctly used and this dust is very damaging to any kind of machine, especially electronic ones.

Electric and electronic typewriters

If you are using an electric or an electronic typewriter you may have two more alternative methods of correcting an error in addition to the methods previously discussed – it depends on the machine and ribbon you are using. Your machine may have a *self correcting feature*. Provided it has and you are using a correctable ribbon you should follow the instructions in your manual. Essentially what happens is that you, or the machine, back-space to the point of error and the error is typed again. A sticky correcting ribbon literally lifts the ink off the page – and the required correction is inserted. This self-correcting feature only works with a correctable ribbon; if your machine is fitted with another type of ribbon you will only be able to correct mistakes using an eraser, fluid or a cover-up ribbon feature (which works like a correcting ribbon, except that it covers the error and does not remove it from the page).

Electronic typewriters with a visual display of any kind enable you to correct the error on the screen before the machine prints what you want – see your manual for operating instructions.

If you are using a *word processor with a VDU* you will be able to correct errors of almost any kind on the screen by following your manual's instructions. Essentially, you move the cursor to the point of the error and type over it after pressing the required delete key. Using the controls as indicated in the manual it is possible not only to delete letters and words but to delete whole texts and/or move text about as required. The advantages of such a system are that you can 'proof read' off the screen before printing material and once printed the material can be recalled and edited off the screen as required. Routine material can be reworked as needed and personalised letters can be produced easily – the standard part of the letter is blended with the individual detail before and during printing.

Cursor keys

Cursor keys enable a microcomputer or word processor user to move the cursor about the VDU as required. On some microcomputers the keys are marked with arrows indicating which way the cursor is to be moved ↑ indicating up and ← to the left for example. On other machines you have to use the control key with other letters to move the cursor. For example, if you are using the WordStar program you need to use control and the 'e' key to move the cursor up a line or control and the 'x' key to move it down a line. The mode of operation will depend on the machine you are using and only the machine manual can tell you what to do.

4.4 CARBON COPIES

Taking carbon copies is a quick and cheap way of taking a copy of any material produced on a typewriter (or word processor) and up to 6 copies can be taken at a time – although the number and quality will depend on such factors as:

the weight of the carbon/film;
the weight of the paper;
the size and style of the type face;
the pressure with which the keys hit the page.

Carbon paper or film

Carbon paper is available in a range of colours and weights – the weight being determined by the amount of ink on the carbon paper. As a rule, the heavier the weight the more ink and the more copies which can be taken. Some carbon paper is *'once used'* which means just what it says – it is used once and is then thrown away. Carbon paper is cheaper than carbon film but it must be stored away from heat and handled with care – the ink soon smudges and it can crease easily, producing a 'treeing' effect on the copies. If left exposed to heat it curls up.

Carbon film, like carbon paper, is available in a range of colours and weights but the coating is rather like a sponge which only releases the ink on impact. Carbon film is plastic film-backed rather than paper-backed, it is easier to handle, requires less exacting conditions in storage, lasts much longer and does not 'tree' or smudge easily. Its semi-fluid surface means that ink from areas not used 'flows' into those which have been used – so each sheet lasts a long time.

Lightweight typing paper is often used when taking carbon copies – the top copy being a good quality bond paper (70 g/m^2) while the carbon copies are taken on $35-40 \text{ g/m}^2$ paper. If copies have to be sent to individuals it is usual to colour code them, e.g. blue for Mrs Jones, yellow for Mrs Wilson, etc.

The type face should be as clear and as sharp as possible – broad, flat faces do not produce good copies as a rule and they certainly do not allow the production of as many copies as does a sharp face.

The pressure/impact controls on electric/electronic typewriters and word processor printers should be adjusted for high impact (see your manual) while some machines also have a setting to be adjusted for large packs of material. If you are using a manual typewriter, type with an even pressure taking care to ensure a heavier impact than if taking just a top copy. A carbon film ribbon will produce better carbon copies than a heavy duty fabric ribbon.

To take one or more carbon copies
Lay the sheet of paper on which a copy is to be made flat on the desk. Place a suitable sheet of carbon paper/film, carbon side down, on top of the copy sheet (so that the back of the carbon paper/film is towards you). Place another copy sheet on top of the carbon and build up the 'pack' ensuring that the top sheet is your original (probably a better quality paper than the copy sheets).

Insert the pack into the machine – you may have to pull the paper release lever forward on manual typewriters to allow large packs to feed down the back of the roller (platen), while on electric/electronic typewriters or printers you may have to make an adjustment to allow for the pack – see the machine manual.

Producing copies
Type with a firm, even pressure when using a manual machine, or adjust the impact setting when using electric/electronic typewriters or printers. If you are using a typewriter any errors must be corrected both on the top copy and on the individual copies. Insert an erasure shield or piece of scrap paper between the carbon side of each sheet of carbon paper/film and the copy sheet beneath as you correct the error on the top copy before correcting each copy. You must not use coloured correcting paper/ fluid on white copy sheets. If you are using a memory machine or a word processor, edit the text on the screen before running off the copies. It is much quicker to take carbon copies than it is to run off individually printed copies when using a memory machine or word processor – although the quality is not as good.

Separating
If you look at a sheet of carbon paper/film you will probably find that the opposing corners have been cut away. This is to allow you to hold the top and copy sheets of paper and gently shake the sheets of carbon paper/ film out of the 'pack'.

Carbon copy notation

If carbon copies are being sent to individuals it is usual to note this fact on the top and copy sheets. This is usually done at the top of the page, e.g. Copies to: MJT, CGS, REB, CCP (or: cc UEA, EEB, WEP, JVE). If, for some reason, it is not appropriate for the person(s) receiving the top copy to know that copies have been sent to others this notation is typed on the copies only. The information is typed after the top copy has been removed from the machine and the copies are often marked 'NOO' (Not On the Original). Some firms have their own notation.

Increasingly, firms program a word processor or microcomputer to run off as many copies as are required – or photocopy originals.

'No carbon required' paper

NCR paper – (No Carbon Required) is paper treated on the back (the side not being typed on) with a substance which produces a carbon-like image on second or subsequent sheets when typed or written on. Any required corrections can be made as indicated for carbon paper on page 41. Many firms produce packs of forms, e.g. invoice, advice note, delivery note, office copy and warehouse copy so that as the typist/operator types one document she produces the others at the same time. These packs are often fastened at the top – so accurate typing is required because they cannot be corrected unless they are taken out of the machine. Users of memory typewriters or word processors are clearly at an advantage when producing carbon copies.

Back-feeding

Sometimes it is necessary to make corrections or additions to an inside sheet of a set which has been fastened at the top, e.g. in the example just given. To make the necessary additions or corrections:

1. Lift the bail bar of the typewriter and insert a clean sheet of paper into the machine as though you were going to type on it.
2. With the typing/printing towards you, the right way up, place the sheet to be corrected between the clean sheet in the typewriter and the roller (or platen).
3. Turn the roller as though you were going to wind the clean sheet out of the typewriter. As you do so the sheet to be corrected/amended will wind itself into the machine and eventually you will be able to remove your clean sheet from the machine.
4. Use the paper release and/or interliner to align the sheet to be corrected/ amended before making the necessary corrections.

LETTERS

While the increasing use of telecommunications services has reduced the amount of correspondence carried on by letters they still form the backbone of communications between individuals and firms and a well produced letter is an aid to the creation of a good impression. There are basically two kinds of letters – *personal* and *business* and within these kinds there are many methods of presentation used in addition to the use of standard and open punctuation (see pages 26 and 30). The most commonly used general style is fully blocked, with open punctuation (called blocked or flush by some writers). The placement of letters should follow the advice given on pages 37 and 38.

Personal letters

These are letters which individuals send to each other as private persons. Some people consider that to type a letter to a friend is 'not the done thing' and they prefer to write personal letters, but if you want to type your personal letters and learn a little more about letter production in general – read on!

5.1 PARTS OF A LETTER

The salutation is the greeting to a letter and in the case of private letters it is usually very informal – its style depends on the relationship between the sender of the letter and the receiver. Many individuals type 'Dear' and write in the rest of the greeting – or write it all.

The complimentary close (also called *the subscription*) is the final regard with which the writer takes leave of the reader. In private letters its form (like the salutation) will depend on the relationship between the writer and reader – in business it is much more formal.

The signature of the sender is not normally typed on private, personal letters because you would expect the receiver of the letter to be able to identify you. If you do decide to type your name at the foot of a personal letter, turn up 5–8 single lines and type it in the same position as the complimentary close – at the left margin when using the fully blocked style or from the centre of the typing line when using the semi-blocked style.

Postscripts are usually taken to be a sign of confusion or haste and so they are to be avoided if possible. However, if necessary type the letters 'PS' at the left-hand margin at least one blank line below your signature (or your typed name) and then type your postscript.

Open punctuation

When a letter is produced using open punctuation all non-essential punctuation before the first and last words in the letter is omitted. The body of the letter is punctuated as in normal English usage, though initials in names, degrees, qualifications and units of measurement are produced with open punctuation.

Standard punctuation

When letters are produced in standard punctuation the addresses of the sender and the addressee are punctuated as described on page 30, and the reference and date are also punctuated. The salutation is followed by a comma and the body of the letter is fully punctuated. The complimentary close is followed by a comma and the name of the company sending the letter, if included, is fully punctuated. The name of the person sending the letter may be followed by a comma if the designation is given, or a full stop if the designation is not given. If the designation is given it is followed by a full stop. Additional information such as enclosures or postscripts are also punctuated. See also Appendix C.

Address of sender

It is usual to include the sender's address at the head of all letters – no matter what kind (private or business). In English lessons at school you were probably told to write the address in the top right-hand corner, to punctuate each line (see page 30 for standard punctuation) and to start each line a little way in from the start of the last line, but you can type your address in *any* position at the head of a personal or business letter. You can:

    centre each line about the middle of the page or typing line;
    type each line from the centre of the typing line;
    back-space each line from the right-hand margin so that when typed
        each line ends on the right-hand margin (justified);

back-space the longest line from the right-hand margin and type all lines from that point;

type each line from the left-hand margin (much the easiest and quickest!).

Turn up at least 7 single lines (to leave a margin of 25 mm (1 in)) at the top of your sheet before typing your address.

No matter what approach you adopt you can use standard or open punctuation *but*, as in all styles of letters, *you should be consistent within each letter* – i.e. the letter should be all standard punctuation *or* all open punctuation. The postal town may be typed with an initial capital on letters but it *must* be typed all in capitals on the envelope.

Telephone number

Your telephone number can be typed in any convenient position in relation to your address – directly underneath it being as convenient and as easy as any. Include your dialling code if you know it.

Fully blocked style of presentation

The quickest way of typing a letter is to use the fully blocked style. In this style all lines begin at the left margin and it is simply a matter of returning the carriage to begin each line.

Your address and telephone number (if any) should be typed at the left margin.

The date should be typed 1 or 2 blank lines (turn up 2 or 3 single lines) after the address – at the left margin. See also page 242.

The salutation or greeting to the letter should be typed 1 or 2 blank lines (consistently) under the date – also at the left margin.

The body of the letter should begin 1 blank line (turn up 2 single lines) after the salutation and the paragraphs should be in the blocked style. Leave a blank line between the paragraphs when they are typed in single line spacing. (It is usual to type letters in single line spacing.)

The complimentary close is typed one blank line after the final full stop in the letter.

The semi-blocked style of presentation

Many individuals prefer to set out their letters in a style similar to that used in English lessons and they consider that the extra time it takes is worth the effort.

The sender's address is typed in any of the positions described on the previous page other than at the left margin.

The date is typed 1 or 2 blank lines (turn up 2 or 3 single lines) in any position from the centre of the typing line or page after the address or telephone number. It may be typed from the centre of the typing line or page or it may be back-spaced so that when typed it ends flush on the right margin – or in any 'intermediate' position.

The salutation is typed 1 or 2 blank lines (consistently) after the date at the left margin.

The body of the letter is typed using indented paragraphs which begin 1 blank line (turn up 2 single lines) after the salutation. Always leave a blank line between indented paragraphs.

The complimentary close is typed 1 blank line after the final full stop in the letter from the centre of the typing line.

5.2 ENVELOPES

Envelopes should be addressed as indicated on pages 28–32 and it is usual for the style of punctuation to follow that used for the letter.

Exercise 21
Practise producing a personal letter in the fully blocked style – see page 45.
Use a suitable sheet of paper and suitable margins – see pages 37–8.

High Elms
8 Ash Hill
Compton
Wolverhampton
WV2 3RT

Telephone Wolverhampton (0902) 76067

21 February 19..

Dear Gwen

What a super surprise! Auntie Frances today
brought the cardigan for Jonathan to Mom's. It
will be ideal for him in the not too distant
future and although he was not a big baby when he
was born (7 lb 3 oz to us and 3.26 kg to the
doctor) he is thriving and has certainly been
making up for lost time. At his last weighing,
(exactly 3 weeks ago) he was 10½ lb and 21 in
long. Mom says he could pass for 3 months easily.

He's given Mom a new lease of life and she's
spoiling him most of the time as you'd expect!
Actually she's been great - especially since she
found him a lot quieter than yours truly.

We're having Jonathan christened on March 6th - so
I hope his Godparents have strong arms! Thanks
again for your kindness.

Love and best wishes

48

Exercise 22

Type this personal letter in any style. As produced here it is a semi-blocked, punctuated letter (see page 45). Use suitable paper and margins.

123 Newhall Street,
Swindon,
Wilts.
SN99 9XX
Tele: 0793 5075

5th August, 19..

Dear Bill and Doreen,

We were pleased to hear that your move to your new home went according to plan and that the dust has started to settle. At least the weather was kind for you and you didn't have the problems we had when we moved here during last winter. No doubt the coming holiday will give you time to sort out the garden - unless you decide to go away. Have you confirmed your booking - or have you let it go because of the move?

Fay is getting excited at the prospect of going down to the 'van again - it's amazing that she can remember so much from last time. We will be down there from the 16th so if you are in our neck of the woods you can drop in. Sue and David will be there when we go down - talk about getting into a rut! Actually it's great when you want to go out for the evening - no babysitting problems.

Mother and father asked us to say thanks for the anniversary present and to say that they will be writing soon - now that they know where you are.

Love to you both,

Exercise 23
Type this personal letter using any consistent style on a suitable sheet of paper. Leave a blank line before and after the display section. This is a fully blocked, open punctuation letter.

Flat 14
Tower House
104 Newhampton Road West
Halesowen
West Midlands
B63 3AG

18 March 19..

Dear Kathy

This is the last time I will be writing to you from the above address - I've decided to join the ranks of the property owners and I've bought a 'mansion' - it's a semi-detached two bedroomed house at:

16 Church Street
Dudley
West Midlands
DY11 1HF

I'm moving in at the end of next week - Pat's helping me with my odds and ends and Robert's said he will help with the heavy stuff - such as I have. It's not a bad property and it's like the one Val and Derek bought last year only this one's in the 'posher' part of town.

I will be sorry to leave the flat but it's silly paying rent when you can be buying your own - as you kept telling me! Actually I'm not moving too far away and it's nearer work so I'll be saving both time and money.

Look me up when you are in the area. Hope all is well with you and your parents - remember me to them next time you see them.

Love

5.3 BUSINESS LETTERS SENT BY INDIVIDUALS

In addition to producing personal letters to relatives and friends, individuals produce their own business letters from time to time. In order to do this they include the name and address of *the addressee* (the person receiving the letter) at the head of the letter. A formal salutation and complimentary close are needed, and the writer must type his or her name under their signature at the foot of the letter. Some business people consider that to send a letter with a justified right-hand margin is more businesslike than the more personal touch when a letter is sent with a ragged margin.

Fully blocked style

When using the fully blocked style the *inside address* (the name and address of the addressee) is placed at the left-hand margin, 1 or 2 blank lines (turn up 2 or 3 single lines) consistently below the date line. Leave 1 or 2 blank lines (consistently) before the salutation.

At the foot of the letter leave 1 blank line (turn up 2 single lines) after the final full stop before typing the complimentary close. Turn up 5–8 single lines before typing your name at the left hand margin. The space you have turned up is to allow you to sign the letter and you type your name underneath in case the person receiving the letter cannot read your signature.

Semi-blocked style

When using the semi-blocked style, the inside address is typed 1 or 2 blank lines (consistently) below the date line at the left hand margin. Leave 1 or 2 blank lines (consistently) after the inside address before the salutation.

At the foot of the letter leave 1 blank line (turn up 2 single lines) before typing the complimentary close from the centre of the typing line.

To find the centre of the typing line, add the 2 margins together and divide by 2. For example, if your margins are 18 and 88 the middle of the typing line will be $18 + 88 = 106$; 106 divided by $2 = 53$. If your margins are 10 and 65, the middle of the typing line will be $10 + 65 = 75$; 75 divided by $2 = 38$ (if the result is an odd number, go to the highest even number).

Turn up 5–8 single lines before typing your name from the centre of the typing line.

Salutation and complimentary close in business letters

In business letters the salutation and complimentary close are more formal than in private personal letters. *When addressing a firm* (as opposed to an individual at a firm) use Dear Sir or Dear Sirs. *When addressing an individual at a firm* whose name you know, use Dear Mr (name) or Dear Mrs (name) or Dear Miss (name) or Dear Ms (name), e.g. Dear Mr Roberts, Dear Mrs Weston, Dear Miss Turner, Dear Ms Yates. If the individual is a friend you may use their first name, e.g. Dear Barry, Dear Olive.

If you began the letter *Dear Sir(s)* or *Dear Madam*, use *Yours faithfully* for the complimentary close, while if you used any other salutation use *Yours sincerely*.

It is usual to indicate *your status* if you are a women when you type your name at the foot of the letter, e.g. Mary Taylor (Mrs), Fay Jones (Miss).

Enclosures

If anything is included with a letter you should draw the reader's attention to the fact by typing *Enc* (indicating one enclosure) or *Encs* (indicating more than one enclosure) at least one blank line below your typed name at the left hand margin no matter what the style of your letter. You could indicate the number of enclosures, e.g. Encs 4. Enclosures may be indicated using an initial capital letter or all capital letters, e.g. ENC, ENCS. Another method sometimes used to indicate enclosures is to type 3 unspaced hyphens in the left margin on the line(s) mentioning it/them. Use the margin release key and back-space 5 spaces before typing the hyphens – leaving 2 spaces between the last hyphen and the body of the letter.

Attention line

Some firms have a rule that all correspondence must be addressed to the firm and not to individuals at the firm. To ensure that the required individual receives the letter you should type:

For the attention of (name of individual)

or

FOR THE ATTENTION OF (NAME OF INDIVIDUAL)

or

Attention (name of individual)

or

ATTENTION: (NAME OF INDIVIDUAL)

The attention line is placed one blank line below the last line of the inside address at the left-hand margin (turn up 2 single lines). Leave one blank line after the attention line before typing the salutation as usual. Such letters use the salutation Dear Sir(s). Some authorities permit the attention line to be typed, as indicated, one blank line *before* the inside address – leaving one blank line after it.

Private and/or confidential

If the information contained in the letter is private or confidential to the individual named type PRIVATE or CONFIDENTIAL or PRIVATE AND CONFIDENTIAL one blank line below the date line at the left hand margin (no matter what the styles of the letter) leaving one blank line between it and the inside address which follows.

Subject heading

If you want to indicate the subject matter of the letter type a subject heading.

Fully blocked style. In the fully blocked style, type the subject heading at the left margin one blank line (turn up 2 single lines) below the salutation. Leave one blank line after the subject heading.

Semi-blocked style. In the semi-blocked style the subject heading is centred about the middle of the typing line – see page 239 for instructions as to centring. Leave one blank line before and one blank line after the subject heading.

Subject headings may be typed all in capitals (in which case they need not be underscored) or with initial capitals (in which case they must be underscored). If the heading requires more than one line type it in single line spacing.

Punctuation

No matter what style of layout is used, all letters may be typed using standard or open punctuation.

Exercise 24

Copy this fully blocked, open punctuation business letter on a suitable sheet of paper.

67 Ingledew Close
Tring
Herts
HP23 5AJ

19 March 19..

The Booking Manager
Holiday Cottages Ltd
6 Rowan Rise
Ripley
Surrey
GU37 6AF

Dear Sir

Thank you for sending me your illustrated brochure and booking information on the cottages you have available in the West of England.

I would like to confirm my telephone call to you earlier today in which I indicated that I want to book The Crow's Nest at Poole for the period 25 August to 8 September. I enclose my cheque for £25 as a non-returnable deposit and note that the balance is due by 15 August.

Thank you for your assistance.

Yours faithfully

Wendy Andrews (Miss)

Enc

Exercise 25
Copy this letter with a subject heading on a suitable sheet of paper.

28 Laburnam Grove   Telephone Skipton 810
Skipton
N Yorkshire
BD23 3RW

9 September 19..

The Production Manager
Commercial and Industrial Printers
33 Ludgate Hill
Shipley
W Yorkshire
BD18 2BS

Dear Sir

ORDER NO 89/023 - COMMEMORATIVE BROCHURE

Please find the corrected proofs of the above
referenced order. I have, as requested, marked
the page proofs in red and blue ink - the former
being your errors and the latter being textual
changes made by me.

Some committee members feel that the reds in the
colour illustrations are not comparable with those
in the photographs submitted. Can you do something about them?

May I remind you that we require delivery by the
first week in October for advertising purposes?

Yours faithfully

Sylvia Yates (Mrs)
Honorary Secretary
Skipton Choral Society

Encs

Exercise 26
Copy this letter on a suitable sheet of paper noting the use of PRIVATE
AND CONFIDENTIAL.

Yew Tree Cottage
50 Bloomfield Road
Worcester
WR1 1JF
Tel: 8989

8 October 19..

PRIVATE AND CONFIDENTIAL

Mr Robert Williams
Williams, George & Willets
Neville House
Stratford Road
Worcester
WR7 2PY

Dear Mr Williams

Enclosed you will find the papers relating to my
father's estate which you requested at our last
meeting. I confirm that you have all the papers
relating to his investments. As you will see from
his bank statement dated 2 February this year he
sold his interest in Security Services plc.

As soon as you have prepared the necessary papers
give me a call and I will arrange to visit your
offices and sign them.

Thank you for your help to date, especially that
concerning the position of the shareholding in
Lefos Plastics Ltd.

Yours sincerely

Wendy Martin (Mrs)

ENCS

56

Exercise 27

Copy this letter on a suitable sheet of paper. Note the use of the attention line and the subject heading.

9 Chantry Drive
Castleton
Derbyshire
S30 2WB
Tel: 340

17 May 19..

Miller, Graham & Co (Midlands)
Summit House
223 Old Park Road
Nottingham
NG2 7QP

Attention: Mr Hughes

Dear Sirs

Ref: 34/107

Thank you for sending me details and application forms for the above referenced post. I now return the application forms for your consideration.

I confirm that I am prepared to undergo a period of residential training in Bristol if selected and that I am available to commence this training in July this year. I enclose the certificates you requested and would be grateful for their early return.

Yours faithfully

Andrew Kent

Encs 3

5.4 BUSINESS LETTERS SENT BY FIRMS

Letters sent by firms follow the layout given for business letters sent by individuals, but because firms need to keep track of letters sent and received it is usual to include some form of identification, *a reference*, at the head of the letter.

Fully blocked letters

The reference to a fully blocked letter is typed at least one blank line below the last line of the printed heading to the sheet. The reference usually consists of the initials of *the signatory* (person signing the letter) and those of the typist who produced the letter. If the letter is one of a series of letters, the initials may be followed by the sequence number, e.g. WE/AR3. Some firms print the word 'Ref' or 'Our ref' on the page and the typist enters the appropriate reference after the printed material (leaving one or 2 spaces between the printed material and the reference). Other firms include a position for the reference of the firm to whom the letter is to be sent – 'Your ref'. Leave 1 or 2 blank lines (turn up 2 or 3 single lines) consistently after the reference before typing the date and the rest of the letter as outlined for private business letters – see page 50.

Semi-blocked letters

As with fully blocked letters, the reference is typed at the left-hand margin. *The date* is typed on the same line as the reference – in any position from the centre of the typing line as described on page 46.

Printed letter heads

To save time and to give a good impression firms print their name and address at the head of the first page of a letter. Styles vary considerably and may include such information as the address of the registered office, telephone and telex numbers, company registration number and even a list of the owners or the products/services offered by the firm. *When typing letters on headed paper* leave at least one blank line between the last line of the printing and the first item – be it a reference or the date. *Some authorities* accept the date typed before the reference in addition to the position outlined above for the fully blocked style. It always appears at the right-hand margin in the semi-blocked style. Some individuals use printed letter heads for all their correspondence.

The designation

The designation or position of the person signing the letter is often included in letters sent by firms. This is typed immediately below the typed signatory in the same position as the signatory.

The name of the organisation sending a letter may be typed at the end of the letter. It is usually typed in capital letters directly under the complimentary close or after the name or designation of the person sending the letter, starting at the same position as the complimentary close, name or designation when using either the fully blocked or the semi-blocked styles. Some authorities accept the name of the organisation typed with initial capital letters.

5.5 CONTINUATION SHEETS

Letters which will not fit on to one sheet of paper have to be continued on other sheets. When producing continuation sheets use sheets of plain paper which are the same size, colour and quality as the top sheet. Use the same margins. To type continuation sheets follow these instructions.

Personal letters
Turn up 4 to 7 single lines and type the page number at the left-hand margin if the style is fully blocked, or in the centre of the typing line if the letter is semi-blocked. Turn up 3 single lines to finish the letter.

Business letters – fully blocked
1. Turn up 4 single lines and type the page number at the left-hand margin.
2. Turn up 2 single lines and type the date, as it appears on the top sheet, at the left-hand margin.
3. Turn up 2 single lines and type the first line of the inside address, as it appears on the top sheet, at the left-hand margin.
4. Turn up 3 single lines to finish the letter, as the example here:

```
2

23 March 19..

Miss Juliana B Olatoye


make a mistake on the wax skin you can correct it
using fluid which - etc.  (See pages 76 and 77.)
```

Business letters – semi-blocked

1. Turn up 4 to 7 single lines (consistently).
2. At the left-hand margin, type the name of the addressee as on the first sheet.

3. Type the page number in the centre of the typing line.
4. Back-space the date from the right-hand margin so that when typed it ends flush on that margin. The date should be typed as it appears on the first sheet.
5. Turn up 3 single lines to continue the letter.

If the first line of the address is a long one and the date is also a long one so that you are short of space you can type the page number in the centre of the typing line and turn up 1 or 2 single lines to type the first line of the address and the date. Examples:

```
Miss Juliana B Olatoye        2       23 March 19..

                              3

Miss Juliana B Olatoye                23 March 19..
```

Leave a margin of 25–30 mm (1–1¼ in) at the foot of the first or subsequent sheets of letters with continuation sheets.

Always carry over a complete line – more if possible – and keep to the style of the first page, fully blocked or semi-blocked, standard or open punctuation.

5.6 LETTERS WITH DISPLAYED MATERIAL

No matter what the style of the letter, fully blocked or semi-blocked, turn up 2 single lines before a displayed section and 2 single lines after a displayed section (to leave a blank line between the section and what goes before or after it).

Fully blocked style
Clear all tabs. From the left margin tap once on the space bar for each letter and space in the longest line in the first column and tap 3 spaces between the first and second columns. Set a tab for the start of the second column. Tap once on the space bar for each letter and space in the longest line in the second column and tap 3 spaces between the second and third columns. Set a tab for the start of the third column. Repeat this process for any other columns. This process can be used for any typewriter or word processor, though you must consult your manual for instructions on how to set the tabs. In the example on page 69, tap:

Cabinets, storage (and 3 spaces). Set a tab.
Digital cassettes (and 3 spaces). Set a tab.

Work across the page, pressing the tabulator to find the starting point of the second and third columns as required.

Semi-blocked style

Clear tabs. Find the middle of the typing line – see page 50. From the middle of the typing line back-space once for every 2 letters and spaces in the longest line in each column and the 3 spaces you should leave between each column. Set a tab at the point reached. From this point tap once on the space bar for each letter and space in the longest line in the first column and the 3 spaces between it and the second column. Set a tab. Tap once for each letter and space in the longest line in the second column and the 3 spaces between it and the third column and set a tab. Continue for any further columns. Each column starts at the point set.

Some electronic typewriters and word processors will automatically display material in columns – see your handbook.

5.7 CIRCULARS

General

Firms, clubs or societies wishing to send out news or information to their clients or members may use circular letters – letters which contain the name of the organisation at the head and the date (which may appear as 'Date as postmark') with a general salutation and the information. Any consistent style of layout may be used for circulars and very often they are duplicated using spirit, ink or offset litho. An example is given on page 80. The signature at the foot of such letters is usually printed with the letter – the person concerned signs the stencil or master before copies are run off.

Personalised circulars

These circulars are, basically, *form letters* and they contain essentially the same information but in order to make them more personal such information as the name and address of the addressee is typed in individually. If a firm has a word processor it will be able to use a *mail merging* program with the letter. The word processor is instructed to print as many copies of the letter as are required while a second program feeds in the individual details of the addressee – name, address and first or second name after the salutation. The impression is thus given that the individual has been sent a personal/individual letter.

Such letters can be duplicated using spirit, ink or offset litho – leaving sufficient space where required for the later insertion of details of the individual. This information should be inserted using a typewriter with the same type style and pitch as the original – but if this is not possible, an obviously different style should be used. If you have to leave space for the later insertion of the date and inside address you should turn up

9-10 single lines between the reference/printed heading and the salutation. See example on page 81.

Letters with return slips
Some firms include a tear-off reply slip for the convenience of their customers.

To produce a tear-off slip, turn up at least 2 single lines after the last item in the letter (designation or enclosure(s)) and type (from edge to edge of the page or margin to margin of the letter) a line using spaced full stops, continuous dots, continuous underscore, spaced hyphens or (author's preference) unspaced hyphens. Turn up at least 2 single lines before typing the form which should be produced in *double line spacing*. If lines are to be included on the form above which information is to be inserted use continuous full stops or the underscore and leave one blank space before the first full stop/underscore as for continuous leader dots – see page 120. An example of a letter with a return slip is on page 82.

62

Exercise 28

Type this letter on a sheet of headed A4 paper. If a suitable sheet is not available make up a suitable address for the head of the sheet.

Our ref DW/BA

14 March 19..

Office Equipment Pty Ltd
Technology House
4 Whyalla Road
PORT ADELAIDE, SA 5015

Dear Sirs

EXPANSION FOR OS34/223 TYPEWRITERS

As one of our major outlets for electronic typewriters we are pleased to give you advance notice of our EX16K units for expanding the capabilities of our OS34/223 machine. This expansion enables the operator to use a full word processing package as and when the need arises. The unit consists of a full screen VDU which enables up to 80 characters to be shown across any document and for 25 lines of material to be displayed down any document. Using scrolling keys the operator is able to check up to 135 characters on any one line and any length of document.

Corrections can be made on the screen and the package includes full word processing capability. The basic memory units store 16 000 characters and can be expanded to 64 000 characters using memory chips. Next year we will be marketing the new DD45 dual disk drive memory units which take double density disks storing 184K per disk - full details later.

We trust that the enclosed package proves of interest to you. Mr Mian, our Sales Manager, will be in touch with you in due course to arrange to visit you and discuss all aspects of this and our other products.

Yours faithfully

Don Wilson
Marketing Manager

Enc

Exercise 29

Set out this letter on a sheet of headed paper – or make up your own heading.

Our ref CY/DAC/1

Your ref NM/PA

15 April 19..

Motor & Machinery Inc
PO Box 40552
Langata Road
NAIROBI
KENYA

Attention: Sales Director

Dear Sirs

NEW MODEL RANGE

As part of our continuing drive to increase our share of the medium and light-weight car market we are pleased to announce that the MLW range will be launched in July. A preview has been arranged for mid-May – full details are enclosed.

Special discounts will be allowed on the first 100 units handled and we think that our pricing policy will permit you to make higher than usual profits. We have a comprehensive advertising package arranged to support the launch.

We trust that you will be able to attend the preview and that you will bring your wife with you. Please contact Mr Olaf Christensen at Head Office if you are able to attend – he will make all the travel and hotel arrangements. We look forward to seeing you.

Yours faithfully

Clive York
Sales Director

Enc

Exercise 30

Set out this letter on a suitable sheet of headed paper – or make up your own heading.

Our ref GSA/WT

9 February 19..

Mr Ibrahim A Safana
Chief Buyer
Office Equipment Ltd
91 Abakpa Way
PMB 2251
KADUNA
NIGERIA

Dear Mr Safana

NEW RANGE OF OFFICE EQUIPMENT

I have much pleasure in sending you our new Office Equipment catalogue which details our entire product range for the coming year. As you will see, we have expanded our range of office copiers and mailing equipment and introduced a new range of electronic document transmission equipment.

We can offer you a service which is second to none and we guarantee to hold prices at the levels indicated in section 9 of the catalogue. We offer extended credit facilities for bulk orders – details on request. Our technical advice section is on 24 hour call for emergencies at any time during the year.

We will, in due course, be sending you packages of leaflets outlining all our products. If you would care to send us your mailing list we can mail direct for you.

Yours sincerely

George S Andersen
Director

Enc

Exercise 31

Set out the letter correctly on a suitable sheet of paper.

Our ref BSM/JLW   Today's date
Mr Alan Y Jefferies, Publishing Services Inc, PO Box 678, Aberdeen, Hong Kong.
Dear Alan, Thank you for the manuscripts you sent for our evaluation and for the books on information technology. As soon as I have chance to have a look at them and send them through the usual channels I will let you have a decision. (Paragraph) By way of returning the compliment I enclose a couple of items which might interest you - they have taken off in a big way over here and are in our Top 10. The book Computers in Education has been written by a team working with Wessex University and several programmers actually teaching at colleges.. The programs can be copied by readers or they can buy the disks. We have found that schools and colleges have gone for it in a big way while home user sales have been excellent. (Paragraph) Future Communications by J A Elkington has done almost as well as Computers in Education. It seems to have a fairly wide appeal and will not require adapting for your markets. (Paragraph) I was sorry to miss you when you were over here last month but I was in the USA for a week in New York. John Winckler asked me to remind you that he will be in Hong Kong next month and he hopes to be able to drop in and see you.
Yours sincerely
Barry S MacKenzie
Publisher Higher Education Division
Encs

Exercise 32

Set out this letter correctly on a suitable sheet of paper. Mark it CONFIDENTIAL.

Our ref HDW/ERT   Today's date
Mr R P Griffiths, Personnel Manager, Roberts & Flack Pty Ltd, Sydney House, Dale Street, Fitzroy, 3867
Dear Mr Griffiths

<u>Miss Wendy Hughes</u>

Thank you for your recent enquiry concerning the above named person who was employed by us as a Sales Person/Receptionist until a month ago. (Paragraph) I am happy to support her application to join your company and would advise that we always found her to be very hard working and reliable in every respect. We employed her straight from college where, as you will see from her application, she had an excellent record. We sent her to our training section after a probationary period with us and she was the outstanding person on the course. She went with our sales team to several Trade Fairs at home and abroad and her facility in French and German was particularly useful. (Paragraph) We made several efforts to keep her in our employment but she is marrying in the near future; her future husband lives in your area and they are buying a house just outside Fitzroy. I think you would be wise to seriously consider employing her.

Yours sincerely

Henry D Watson
Personnel Manager

Exercise 33

Set out this letter correctly on a suitable sheet of paper.

Ref: RT/PEC
Today's date
Modern Furnishings plc, 34 High Street, King's Lynn.   PE30 1PB
Attention: Mr E Walters
Dear Sirs
Your order 34/891
I regret that it will not be possible to supply the curtain material specified in the above referenced order which arrived earlier today. You may recall that when we supplied the last order of this particular material we advised that it was a special offer designed to clear our warehouse and that we could not guarantee further supplies. (Paragraph) This particular line is imported by us from the Far East and whilst the fabric is of uniform quality the dyes vary slightly from batch to batch. We have completely sold out of that particular batch and despite several requests from other customers we have been unable to obtain further supplies. In the latest shipment we have received the only slight difference is in the golds - which are a fraction more yellow than those in the previous order. (Paragraph) I have taken the liberty of sending you a sample of the latest batch for your consideration and suggest that unless you have to match exactly it is a good substitute. I can offer you extensive stocks of this material but would repeat my earlier comments about the dyes varying from shipment to shipment.
Yours faithfully
Robert Tillings
Sales Manager   Enc

68

Exercise 34

Set out this letter on a suitable sheet of paper. Head the letter GIFT CATALOGUE (next year).

Our ref NHJ/ER   Today's date

Mr Christopher Prior, Manager, The Gift Shop, Hayle, Cornwall.   TR27 5BH

Dear Mr Prior

Thank you for your letter of (dated 4 days ago) enquiring about suitable items for sale during the coming season. I have pleasure in sending you our latest illustrated catalogue. (Paragraph) I would draw your attention to page 7 - pens with built-in LCD digital watches. These pens take a standard 'Parker' refill and display hours, minutes and seconds or the month and day. They are accurate to half a minute per month and the more expensive version includes an alarm and hourly chimes. We can engrave these pens with the name of your resort or, for a small handling charge, engrave the name of the purchaser. They have proved to be very popular during the past year. (Paragraph) On pages 178-83 you will find a range of casual and formal bags and these can be supplied in a range of motifs. They are particularly attractive because of the wide price range. On pages 23-30 we offer a clearance range of cameras. These are discontinued lines which we are offering at well below cost price so that you should be able to make a substantial profit on them. They are fully covered by the manufacturers' guarantees, and as you will see, they are well-known makes. (Paragraph) If you require any further information please contact us on Freefone 3498 or use the Freepost envelope enclosed. Yours sincerely HOLIDAY MERCHANDISE LTD   Norman H Johnson, Sales Director   Encs

Exercise 35
Copy this fully blocked letter with a display section on a suitable sheet
of headed paper. Set out the display correctly – see page 59.

Our ref: JI/NC1

6 April 19..

Mr John R Franklin
Units 39/40
Bondeni Industrial Park
FOOTSCRAY 3011
AUSTRALIA

Dear Mr Franklin

I was pleased to learn that our publicity has reached the Antipodes
and that you are interested in our mail order service. We carry a
vast range of office and microcomputer supplies and accessories as
you will see from the new catalogue I am sending you this month
when the new edition arrives from the printer. There is little
point in sending you the old edition! To keep you happy I enclose
current leaflets on the following - a small part of our total
range.

Binders	Digital cassettes	Racks
Cabinets, storage	Dust covers	Ribbons
Cable holders	Furniture	Rulers/templates
Carrying cases	Glare filters	Turntables
Cleaning kits	Hub rings	VDU stands
Copyholders	Modems	Wallboards
Daisy wheels	Paper	Wallplates
Data cartridges	Print wheels	Wire trays

Once we have suitable bank references we can supply on telex orders
and despatch goods within 12 hours of receipt. We are prepared to
offer discounts for bulk purchases - details in the catalogue.

I enclose full details of our trading conditions and will be happy
to deal with any questions you might have in the future.

Yours sincerely
OFFICE AND COMPUTER SUPPLIES INC

Joe Inmac
Sales Director

Encs

Exercise 36

Copy this fully blocked letter with a display section on a suitable sheet of headed paper as for despatch today – insert today's date.

Our ref RD/IAS

The Sales Manager
International Computers Inc
Lehigh Valley
PENNSYLVANIA 18995
USA

Dear Sir

SERVICE CENTRES FOR THE RAS RANGE

I would advise that servicing facilities have been established at
the addresses below. These are in addition to those listed in the
manuals sent with the last consignment.

RAS Service	RAS Service	RAS Service
542 Ploenchit Road	J Tata Road	Casilla 678
BANGKOK	BOMBAY 20	SANTIAGO DE CHILE
THAILAND	INDIA	CHILE
RAS Service	RAS Service	RAS Service
2873 Lapierre Street	Apartado 61	23 Market Street
LASALLE/QUEBEC H8N 1B7	MADRID	PRAHRAN 3183
CANADA	SPAIN	AUSTRALIA
RAS Service	RAS Service	RAS Service
17 Kanta Road	PO Box 876	PO Box 126
KADUNA	KARACHI 4	El-Molo Street
NIGERIA	PAKISTAN	NAIROBI
		KENYA

Can you please insert these addresses (copies enclosed) in the last
batch of manuals we sent? The new edition will have them printed
with our existing service centres.

Yours sincerely

Roy Dean
SERVICING MANAGER

Encs

Exercise 37

Copy this semi-blocked letter with a display section on a suitable sheet of headed paper – see page 60.

Our ref VAG/RT1   Today's date

Mrs R A Bakari
Office Supervisor
BML Ltd
34 Canton Road
HONG KONG

Dear Mrs Bakari

                    YOUR LETTER DATED (six days ago)

    I thank you for your recent letter in which you asked about the $5\frac{1}{4}$" flexible disks we supply for the microcomputers you listed. As you will see from the enclosed leaflet, our disks are guaranteed for life. The disk types about which you enquired are as follows.

Manufacturer	Drive Model	Disk Type
AES	Plus	W
Apple IIe	Pascal	Z
Atari	400/500	Z
Honeywell	M4108	ZZ
IBM	Series 500	ZZ
Nexos	2200	AA

    The Wang Wangwriter uses 8" Type YY disks while the Xerox-820 uses 8" Type Z disks. All disks are supplied in boxes of 10 and can be despatched the same day as ordered.

    I have taken the liberty of sending you an order form and look forward to hearing from you soon. Repeat order forms are automatically included with completed orders.

                              Yours sincerely

                              Victor A George
                              Sales Manager

Encs

Exercise 38

Set out the letter on a suitable sheet of paper. Take one carbon copy and at the top left-hand margin of the carbon only type: File OS/45A. Type the names in one column only.

Ref TBV/wS/3/C   19 May 19..

Ms Elizabeth Lautenschlager, Makindu Growers & Packers Ltd, Box 10782, MOMBASA, KENYA. Dear Ms Lautenschlager, I confirm that a party of 6 from our Company will be visiting you the week commencing 23 June. They will arrive at the airport on Flight No 789/34A at 0945 hrs and travel to the International Hotel by hire car. I have arranged for them to have dinner with you in the evening and you can finalize the arrangements for their tour of your enterprise after dinner. The members of the party will be:

Mr Andrew Jenkins, Managing Director   Mr John H Marsh, Chief Accountant
Miss Susan Oldfield, Advertising   Mrs Valerie A Marshall, Company Secretary
Mr Bob Turner, Sales Director   Mr Ian White, Production Manager

Mr Marsh and Mrs Marshall will be particularly concerned with the financial side of our proposed venture, Miss Oldfield and Mr Jenkins will be looking at possible advertising campaigns while Mr Turner and Mr White will want to discuss processing and distribution. I think that we have agreed upon most of the points you raised and anticipate that contracts can be signed at the end of the visit. (Paragraph) May I thank you and your Board for being so frank and prompt in your dealings with us to date. I look forward to meeting you again when I join the party at the end of the visit to sign contracts.
Yours sincerely   Trevor B Vadgama   Company Chairman

Exercise 39

Set out the letter on a suitable sheet of paper. Take one carbon copy and mark the copy: Mr Wilson – for file.

Your ref OM/PY   Our ref CD/JSN   Today's date
Fashion Fabrics plc, 60-62 Wilbury Way, Leeds. LS2 8NG
For the attention of Mrs W Markham

Dear Sirs, Thank you for your above referenced letter which reached us on (5 working days ago from the date of this letter). We can supply the materials about which you asked and would advise you that we also specialise in top quality silks in the following ranges and colours – samples enclosed together with price lists.

Eastern Range	Oriental Range	Pacific Range	Indian Range
Fig Green	Bronze	Amber	Emerald
Lemon	Brown	Aquamarine	Flame
Rose-Pink	Cobalt	Blue	Ivory
Scarlet	Crimson	Mauve	Orange
Yellow	Purple	White	Vermilion

Your order is currently being made up and will be despatched later today together with the woollen suiting samples about which you also enquired recently. The new season's stock has just arrived and I would advise that generally prices are the same as last year – details enclosed with the samples. (Paragraph) I trust you will find the silks of interest and look forward to your comments on them.
Yours faithfully   Cathleen Dawson   Sales Supervisor   ENCS

Exercise 40

Set out this fully blocked letter with continuation sheet(s) – see page 58.
Take one carbon copy.

Your ref HIF/EE

Our ref WRM/AW

Mr Keith Lloyd
Office Manager
Bennett & Williams plc
65a Regent Street
Guildford
Surrey
GU4 8QZ

Dear Mr Lloyd

WORD PROCESSOR SYSTEMS

Thank you for your above referenced letter - I can well understand
your frustration and confusion. I can only hope that what follows
is of assistance.

WORD PROCESSORS

Almost any microcomputer which has a printer attached is capable of
being used in the production of a wide range of 'typed' material.
A dedicated word processor is a machine with a large memory, a VDU
(Visual Display Unit) and a high quality (daisy wheel, thimble or
golf ball) printer which is designed for one function only - word
processing. Most 'dedicated' word processors will, in fact, perform a range of functions such as stock control or wages. To my
mind to be entirely satisfactory you require a screen which will
show you at least a whole page of A4 paper without scrolling; a
memory of over 350K per drive (you need dual drives); a high speed
printer offering a range of type styles (metal wheels rather than
plastic daisy wheels) and a range of stations for inputting.
Dedicated word processors (like micros with a word processing
program - see later) use a program to tell the operator what to do
to perform a range of tasks. Depending on the program used it
takes from a few hours to a couple of days to train the operator -
most programs have a 'help' key if anything goes wrong. A top
quality word processing system costs a lot of money but it does a
lot of work. Many have communications capability.

MICROCOMPUTERS

As indicated earlier, most microcomputers can perform a word
processing function provided they are given a printer and a
program. There is a vast range of programs available including WordStar, Superscript, Applewriter - and so on. The
information is displayed on a VDU but most VDUs will only show
up to 80 characters across a page and 24-25 lines of text down
a page. You can scroll across or up and down a page of any
conventional size as required. The word processing program

may be one of several available for the micro - the range
offered depends on the machine you opt for. One problem with
some micros is that they simply do not have the memory required for adequate word processing while another can be the
problem of interfacing with a good printer. You may find,
however, that a micro with a hard disk and a suitable printer
is a cheaper option than a dedicated word processor - and it
will probably give you a wider range of programs to run.

WORD PROCESSING TYPEWRITERS

Some typewriter manufacturers sell word processing systems
which consist of a typewriter with a limited VDU (often under
20 characters) and disk storage. The operator edits off the
screen and stores material on disks (they come in a range of
sizes and storage capacities). The advantages of such systems
is their low cost, the fact that you can use them as typewriters for small tasks and the fact that some can perform a
limited range of additional tasks such as stock control and
wages. Powerful machines have, like some word processors and
some micros, a communications function - you type the material
in at your end and out it comes wherever you have an appropriate terminal. (Paragraph) The problem with most word processing typewriters is their limited memory. Many salesmen will
tell you that 16K or 32K is all you need - but the former will
only give you about 4 pages of A4 text and the latter double
this amount. Much will depend on your line spacing and the
size of print you want to use. (Paragraph) From your letter
I would suggest that you take a look at a large memory micro
with a VDU and an electronic typewriter which you can use as a
printer. Make sure that they have an RS232 interface. I have
sent you a range of leaflets and will call to see you soon.
Yours sincerely   William R Markham
Office Systems Consultant   Encs 12

Exercise 41

Set out this fully blocked letter on suitable sheets of paper – see page 58 for continuation sheets. Make up your own first address.

Our ref BT/ES

23 March 19..

Miss Juliana B Olatoye
Design Group Nigeria
Ahmadu Bellow Way
KADUNA
NIGERIA

Dear Miss Olatoye

OFFICE DUPLICATORS

I thank you for your recent enquiry about office duplicators
and will try to answer the questions you asked. I have taken
the liberty of sending you a collection of leaflets showing
the current models together with a list of our stockists.

SPIRIT (HECTOGRAPHIC) DUPLICATORS

The system uses a master sheet which is made up using a range
of 7 colours of carbon sheets. The master sheet is a
specially treated bond paper with a china clay coating. The
coating side is placed on the carbon side of the chosen
coloured sheet and information is typed or written on the
back. Any corrections have to be made by removing the carbon
from the reverse side of the master sheet and this can be done
with a sharp knife or using special paint-out fluid. You must
use a separate carbon sheet for each chosen colour. When your
master has been made to your satisfaction it is fastened to
the steel roller of the duplicating machine. As sheets of
duplicating paper are fed through the machine a small quantity
of the carbon is washed off the master by special alcohol and
it is deposited on to the duplicating sheet which emerges
slightly damp from the machine. Up to 200 copies can be taken
from each master which can be stored as required. The main
advantages of this system are its low cost and its colours.

INK DUPLICATORS

Ink duplicators use a stencil which you can prepare in a
variety of ways - usually on a typewriter of some kind. You
must select a suitable stencil for your particular machine.
The master consists of a wax skin and a backing sheet. As you
write/type on the wax skin you produce 'holes' through which
ink can pass from the duplicator on to duplicating paper as it
passes through the machine. You can correct errors by
painting them over using correcting fluid. You can run off
copies in 2 colours but you will need a separate stencil for
each colour and 2 duplicators - either that or you will have
to wash out your machine each time you change the colour. You
can run off up to 2000 copies from each stencil.

OFFSET LITHO

This method uses a master sheet which can be made of paper or
metal. You can write on this master using special pens or
type using a litho ribbon in your typewriter - there is a vast
range of colours available. Care must be taken to keep the
master free from dirt and grease - especially when making
corrections. This system enables copies to be run off using a
range of papers and almost any colour - the number of copies
from a metal plate are almost limitless.

Spirit and ink duplicators come in a wide range of machines
ranging from simple hand operated low-cost machines to those
using the latest micro-chip technology. Price, naturally,
increases with the complexity of the machine.

Offset litho machines also come in a wide range of sizes and
all are electrically operated. In general they are far more
expensive than the other 2 kinds of duplicators but then they
offer a great many more facilities. (Paragraph) No matter
which system you opt for I can assure you that they are all
extremely reliable and they require the minimum of mainten-
ance. In view of your letter I would advise you to take a
very careful look at spirit or ink duplicators. I think, from
what you say, that you will be able to undertake all the jobs
you described on either of these.   Yours sincerely
Barry Thomas   Duplicating Sales Manager   ENCS

Exercise 42
Set out this letter in the semi-blocked style and take a continuation
sheet. Use a suitably headed sheet for the first sheet. See page 59.

Our ref HKL/RY/NC   19 May 19..

Mr Robert Angaine
Monotype Printers Ltd
60 Independance Square
PO Box 718
Port-of-Spain
TRINIDAD

Dear Mr Angaine

                    INTERNAL TELEPHONE SYSTEMS

        Thank you for your interesting letter dated 12 May in
which you enquired about the range of internal telephone
systems we manufacture and export. We pride ourselves on
being world market leaders in this field and can supply, and
fit if required, any communications system in any part of the
world. From your letter it would seem that our SCRA System 5
or our SCRA System 7 would best suit your particular needs.

SCRA SYSTEM 5

        This system does not require a switchboard operator yet
it offers an internal telephone service and a public exchange
service at the extensions. It is available in 2 sizes: with
capabilities of up to 3 exchange lines and 10 extensions or
with up to 5 exchange lines and 20 extensions. (Paragraph)
Any number of the extensions can be made designated extensions
- a designated extension is one which can be used to answer
incoming exchange line calls and transfer them, if required,
to other extensions. Calls can be made between extensions by
dialling the required number. The system has the facility to
be linked to other SCRAXs (Small Call Routing Apparatus
Exchanges) which may be manually or automatically operated.
(Paragraph) Incoming exchange calls ring bells near the
designated extensions and any of them can answer by picking up
the receiver. The incoming call can then be transferred to
another extension by pressing a button on the telephone,

dialling the required number and replacing the receiver as
soon as the call is accepted. The call can be regained by the
designated extension by pressing the button on the telephone.
(Paragraph) If the transfer does not take place for any
reason the incoming call rings the bells again and any
designated extension can take the call by lifting the handset.
A designated extension can interrupt an engaged extension to
advise of an incoming call by dialling 1. A ticking sound
warns of the intrusion.

SCRA SYSTEM 7

This system requires an operator but it meets the
requirements of organisations requiring up to 20 exchange
lines and 100 extensions. The operator receives incoming
exchange calls on the press button switchboard and connects
the extensions as required. (Paragraph) Internal calls can
be made by dialling directly from one to another using any of
the numbers from 200 to 299. Exchange calls can be made
direct from automatic extensions by dialling 9 to get an
exchange line. The SCRA operator can interrupt a call on an
engaged extension to ask if another call can be accepted - a
ticking sound warns the extension user that the operator is on
the line.

NIGHT SERVICE FACILITIES

Both systems offer night service facilities. When the
button on the telephone/switchboard is pressed any suitably
sited bells ring as soon as an incoming call is received.
(Paragraph) We provide a wide range of telephones with both
systems and the choice is up to the user. Power supplies for
the internal telephones are provided using mains electricity,
that from your own generators or, in the event of a power
failure, batteries. External calls will be cut off in the
event of a power failure on the part of the telephone company.
(Paragraph) We are prepared to lease either system and both
leasing and direct purchase prices are subject to foreign
currency fluctuations. Enclosed you will find full technical
specifications of both systems and service contracts. I look
forward to hearing from you. Yours faithfully
Henry K Laval   Marketing Manager   ENCS 9

Exercise 43
Type this general circular on a suitable sheet of headed paper – see page 60.

Ref EWN/AJC

Date as postmark

Dear Sir/Madam

Thank you for your recent enquiry concerning the Universal microcomputer system. I hope that from the enclosed leaflets you are able to obtain a greater understanding of the Universal system and its suitability for use within a small business.

Your local Universal dealer will only be too happy to offer further information and advice on the range of accessories that make the Universal the most versatile microcomputer currently available for small business use. A list of all the dealers in our network is enclosed.

Included in the software booklet you will find details of programs which will enable you to make fullest use of your Universal system from the outset. Whilst many business owners are keen to write their own programs others find that our comprehensive range saves them this burden.

The Universal system carries an unconditional 1 year guarantee and our dealers offer competitive service contracts after that time.

Yours faithfully

Eric W Nevil
Sales Manager Universal Computers

Encs 4

Exercise 44

Type this personalised circular on a suitable sheet of headed paper. Leave space for the later insertion of the date and inside address – see page 60.

Dear

SPECIAL OFFERS TO EXISTING CUSTOMERS

Last year we kept our prices stable and until (2 month's time) we are having a special promotion which involves only our existing customers. During this period you will be entitled to a 'Special Customer Discount' of 15% off our list prices for orders placed at the time of quotation. This is a thank you from us to you for your past support.

I am pleased to announce the opening of our Showroom in (make up a suitable address). Here we have examples of our entire product range in home settings. You are cordially invited to visit and celebrate with us in our new venture any day from Monday to Saturday. If you require any further information please forward the pre-paid card (enclosed), contact any of our staff at Head Office or pay us a visit at our Showroom.

May I take this opportunity to remind you of our 'Personal Recommendation Commission'. To cut costs we limit our advertising and rely on customers to introduce us to their family and friends. In return we will pay you a fee equal to 10% of orders placed with us and you can either keep this as a thank you from us to you or you can share it with your family and friends.

I thank you for your custom in the past and look forward to you visiting our Showroom.

Yours faithfully

Herbert Roberts
Financial Director

Enc

82

Exercise 45

Type this circular with a tear-off slip on a suitable sheet of headed paper - see page 61.

Date as postmark

Dear Member

HOTEL CATERING

While we all enjoy staying in a hotel or going out for a meal few realise how much hard work goes into ensuring that these occasions go smoothly. Your committee has arranged for a behind the scenes look at the kitchens of The Continental Hotel in Exhibition Road for its next monthly venture.

The visit starts at 1730 hrs on (date in 6 weeks' time) when staff will be preparing the evening meal. You will see meals being prepared and after the tour you will dine in the Paris Suite. If you want to join the visit please complete the attached slip and return it to the secretary (address above).

Yours sincerely

David Malik
Chairman

I (name) _____

of (address) _____

_____

would like to go on the hotel visit.

Membership number _____

Signature _____

Exercise 46

Set out this general circular on a suitably headed sheet of paper.

Our ref LSA/RTA

March (this year)

Dear Enquirer

We thank you for your enquiry regarding our range of Hi-Fi equipment and have much pleasure in enclosing a booklet which describes the specifications of the equipment we manufacture. We aim to cater for the person who wants to listen to the best available sound and the casual listener who wants to hear music on a budget. (Paragraph) As you will see from the booklet, we aim to provide equipment which is easy on the eye as well as easy on the ear (and the pocket!) and gives you, the user, the maximum flexibility in building up a package which suits your particular needs. We provide, through our dealer network, a comprehensive service and try to help you obtain the most suitable equipment for your particular situation. We boast that we tailor our equipment to your home and you are free to try modules in your home before purchase. Our dealers will only be too happy to advise you. (Paragraph) You will note that we offer several attractive packages which show a significant reduction over buying separate items. All our equipment is covered by our 12 months unconditional guarantee and any items which are returned within 2 weeks of purchase will be refunded in full - or you can put the money towards other equipment.

Yours sincerely

HI-FI SOUNDS

Larry S Anderson

Sales Support Manager

Enc

84

Exercise 47

Type this personalised circular on a suitable sheet of headed paper. Leave space for the later insertion of the date and inside address.

Dear

PROCESSED FOODS AND THEIR EFFECTS UPON GENERAL HEALTH

I wish to draw your attention to a booklet which we have recently published - Processed Foods and their effects upon general health. The aim of this booklet is to educate and inform both you, the consumer, and us, the manufacturers' association about processed foods and possible health effects. Our association represents an industry which affects just about every man, woman and child in the country - all of whom purchase and consume processed food of some kind. (Paragraph) From time to time various agencies seek to criticise our products in the areas of nutrition and dental health and we, for our part, seek to liaise with all parties to ensure that all such adverse comment is resolved. Part of our booklet seeks to deal with these aspects and suggests that much of this criticism has been facile and misinformed. (Paragraph) If you would like any further information about any aspect of our association please let me know and I shall be delighted to assist. If you feel that you could assist us by taking part in our regular surveys I shall be delighted to hear from you.

Yours sincerely

Robert Johnson

Chairman Processed Foods Association

Exercise 48

Set out this circular with a tear-off slip correctly on a suitable sheet of headed paper – see page 61. Use any suitable date.

Dear Customer

CASUAL FASHIONS

I am delighted to hear that you want a free copy of our fully illustrated Casual Fashions catalogue which you will find enclosed. Our policy has always been to provide you, the customer, with real value for money – top quality styling and the best available materials. (Paragraph) In order to cut our prices to the bone we only deal direct with you, the public. We boast that we are the only firm to offer quantity discounts and the more you buy the more we knock off the bill. This is coupled with our no-nonsense guarantee – if you are not completely satisfied return the goods within 48 hours and you get ALL your money back. (Paragraph) If you would like your friends to hear about us please fill in the attached slip and we will rush them their free copy of our catalogue. Help us to help you – the more we sell the better value you get. Please return the slip in the postage paid envelope.

Yours sincerely

Sally Weaver

Sales Director

Please rush my friend(s) a copy of your super Casual Fashions Catalogue.

Name _____

Address _____

Name _____

Address _____

Name _____

Address _____

Use the back for any more names and addresses!

DISPLAYS

Displays may be set out either in the blocked or the centred style.

6.1 BLOCKED STYLE

In the blocked style all the material is typed from the left-hand margin. Users of some electronic typewriters and users of word processors will be able to display material automatically following the manual instructions. Lesser mortals will have to work out each individual display!

To display material on any page using equal margins top and bottom and on each side of the page in the blocked style:

1. Clear margins and tabs.
2. Measure the paper to find the middle of its width. (Fold and 'nick' it or measure and lightly mark the centre point with a pencil.)
3. Move the typing point to the centre of the page.
4. Choose the longest line in the display. In Example 1 it is 'Pacific Prawn Cocktail'.
5. Back-space *once* for *every 2 letters and spaces* in the longest line in the display. Set a left margin at the point reached. In Example 1 back-space one letter for each group: Pa ci fi cspace Pr aw nspace Co ck ta il. (Had there been an odd letter you would have ignored it.)
6. Find the middle of the depth of the page – using same procedure as finding the middle of the width.
7. Put the paper into the machine at 0 on the scale on the left or balance it about the centre of the bail bar scale (on some machines the scale is 0 to the width of the platen, while on others it is 0 in the middle of the platen). Line up the mid-point in the markings on the card holder.
8. Turn the roller anticlockwise (as though winding the paper back out of the machine) one 'click' for each line and each space down the display. (Each click is a half line space on machines offering 6 lines of type to

25 mm (1 in).) The spacings in the following example are only a guide and you can choose your own spacings provided that there is space for the display down the page. In the example below click:

1 (M E N U); 2 (blank line); 3 (blank line); 4 (Iced Melon); 5 (or); 6 (Pacific Prawn Cocktail); 7 (blank line); 8 (Roast Chicken); 9 (or); 10 (Roast Sirloin of Beef); 11 (or); 12 (Deep Fry Scampi); 13 (blank line); 14 (Choice of Vegetables); 15 (or); 16 (Choice of Salad); 17 (blank line); 18 (Fresh Fruit); 19 (or); 20 (Various Ices); 21 (blank line); 22 (blank line); 23 (Tea or Coffee).

This is the point at which you begin typing. All lines are typed from the left margin. See also page 88 for turning up.

Example 1
Display the menu about the centre of a sheet of A5 (148 × 210 mm) paper with equal margins top and bottom and on each side of the page following the instructions given earlier.

```
        M E N U
        2 blank lines

        Iced Melon
        or
        Pacific Prawn Cocktail
        blank line
        Roast Chicken
        or
        Roast Sirloin of Beef
        or
        Deep Fry Scampi
        blank line
        Choice of Vegetables
        or
        Choice of Salad
        blank line
        Fresh Fruit
        or
        Various Ices
          2 blank lines

        Tea or Coffee
```

To type the display on the previous page

1. Type M E N U at the left margin.
2. Return the carriage 3 times to leave the required 2 blank lines and type 'Iced Melon'.
3. Return the carriage and type 'or'.
4. Return the carriage and type 'Pacific Prawn Cocktail'.
5. Return the carriage twice to leave the required blank line.

Continue until the Menu is complete. REMEMBER: to leave *one blank line* between items you must return the carriage *twice*. To leave *2 blank lines* between items you must return the carriage *3 times* - in other words, you must turn up one more blank line than the number of spaces you want to leave between lines. If you wanted to leave 5 blank lines for some reason you would turn up 6 lines.

6.2 CENTRED STYLE

In the centred style all lines are individually centred about the middle of the page or typing line as appropriate. This can be done automatically on some electronic typewriters and on all word processors - see your manual.

To display material in the centred style using equal margins top and bottom and with each line centred:

1. Clear all margins and tabs.
2. Find the middle of the width of the paper. (Fold and 'nick' it or measure it and lightly mark the centre point with a pencil.)
3. Set a tab at the middle of the page.
4. Find the middle of the depth of the page - in the same way as you found the middle of the width.
5. Put the paper into the machine at 0 on the scale on the left, or balance it about the centre of the bail bar (see also page 86).
6. Turn the roller anticlockwise (as though winding the paper back out of the machine) one 'click' for each line of typing and each space down the display. (Each click is half a line space on machines offering 6 lines of type to 25 mm (1 in).) The spacings given in Example 2 are only a guide and you can choose any spacings provided the display will fit down the page. In the example given, click: 1 (SEE); 2 (blank line); 3 (GUYS AND GALS); 4 (blank line); 5 (F R E E F A S H I O N SHOWS); 6 (blank line); 7 (daily); 8 (blank line); 9 (1130 hrs and 1630 hrs); 10 (blank line); 11 (in the); 12 (blank line); 13 (MARKET HALL); 14 (blank line); 15 (blank line); 16 (THIS WEEK ONLY!).

This is the point at which you begin typing.

Example 2

Display the invitation about the centre of a sheet of A5 (210 × 148 mm) paper with equal margins top and bottom of the sheet and with each line centred. Follow the instructions given.

SEE

blank line

GUYS AND GALS

blank line

F R E E   F A S H I O N   S H O W S

blank line

daily

blank line

1130 hrs and 1630 hrs

blank line

in the

blank line

MARKET_HALL

2 blank lines

THIS WEEK ONLY!

To type the display

1. Press the tab bar and find the middle of the width of the page.
2. Back-space once for every 2 letters in the line. Back-space SE and ignore the odd letter E. Type 'SEE'.
3. Return the carriage twice to leave the required blank line.
4. Press the tab bar and find the middle of the width of the page.
5. Back-space once for every 2 letters and spaces in the line. Back-space GU YS spaceA ND space G AL. Ignore the odd letter S. Type 'GUYS' AND GALS'.
6. Return the carriage twice to leave the required blank line.
7. Press the tab bar to find the middle of the width of the page.
8. Back-space once for every 2 letters and spaces in the line. Back-space: Fspace Rspace Espace Espace spacespace Fspace Aspace Sspace Hspace Ispace Ospace Nspace spacespace Sspace Hspace Ospace Wspace and ignore the odd letter S. Type the line and finish the display as indicated.

Calculation of top and bottom margins – alternative method

1. Calculate the number of lines of type available down the sheet of paper. Most typewriters give 6 lines of type to 25 mm (1 in) down a sheet of paper, but some give up to 8. Consult your machine handbook.

2. Calculate the number of lines the display will occupy on the page.
3. Take the number of lines occupied by the display from the number of lines down the page.
4. Divide the answer by 2 and then add 1. If there is a remainder when you divide ignore it.
5. Put the paper into the machine and turn up the number of lines indicated at point 4 above. Start typing at the point reached.

In the display on the previous page

1. There are 35 lines available down a sheet of A5 paper (210 x 148 mm) using 6 lines of type to 25 mm (1 in).
2. The display occupies 16 lines – see the calculation on page 88.
3. 35 – 16 = 19.
4. 19 divided by 2 = $9\frac{1}{2}$. Call it 9. Add the extra 1. 9 + 1 = 10.
5. Put the paper into the machine and turn up 10 single lines. Centre the first line and continue as outlined earlier.

This method of calculation of top and bottom margins can be used for all forms of display and tabular work. See page 244 for the number of lines of type available down various sized sheets of paper.

Exercise 49
Display each of the following on suitable sheets of paper in the blocked or the centred style following the instructions given on page 86-90.

STOP!

BEFORE YOU RENEW YOUR INSURANCE

LET OUR COMPUTER
WORK FOR YOU

SAFEGUARD INSURANCE BROKERS
High Street
Tele: 7766

BROKE?

we give TOP PRICES

for your second hand

G O L D   A N D   S I L V E R

Call in for FREE ESTIMATE

The Treasure Chest
Hospital Street

Is the woman in your life
tired of cooking for you?

H U R R Y !

Bring her out for a meal and
we will WINE her (and you) for

F R E E

The Eating House
Eastchurch Road - Tele: 8978

Exercise 50

Display each of the following on suitable sheets of paper in the blocked or the centred style. Set them out to your own design – if you are using a word processor use a range of type styles when printing them.

LEAFLET DISTRIBUTION We can circulate up to 25 000 copies each week in this area GET THE FACTS Call 37372

Opening (suitable date) FASHION BOUTIQUE You want it? We're sure to have it! What we don't have we can get for you. For the very latest fashions for both sexes – Lucette House, Riverside Drive. SUPER OPENING OFFERS

AUTO SPARES Vast range of all leading makes. We specialise in ordering for unusual makes – give us a try! Bits and Bobs Golf Course Road. Petrol, Oil and Servicing.

For the lastest in Hi-Fi, Radio and TV – The Audio-Visual Centre, top of the market by the cross roads. BUY or RENT. Wide range of cassettes, tapes and records. Tele: 8979

GLASS? All sizes cut to order. Any weight and colour supplied. Broken windows? We fix them! UNIVERSAL GLASS, South Parade. Ample free parking.

Tired of hunting for the lowest prices? Want the unusual food item? Try us. Walker & Sons, Valley Field Estate East. Beers, Wines and Spirits. Large cheese selection.

MIDLAND METAL CO (founded 1909) Lahore Road Electroplaters, Engravers, Gunsmiths, Engineers, Company Seals, Die Sinkers, Machinists, Founders and Welders, Sheet Metal Workers. Tel 24454 and 25534

DESIGN ARTISTS Signwriters, Van Displays, Commercial Artists, Designers, Gold Leaf Writers, Displays, Plastic Signboards, Colour Slides. D & G GREENHAM, Design House, County Road. Tel 5762

SHIPPING AGENTS Importers of Fertilizers, Phosphates, Refined Sugar, Grains, Oil and Timber. Exporters of manufactured goods. We quote on anything! H T SHIPPING AND FORWARDING CO, Unit 10 Industrial Estate. Tel 87872 or 99334

TABULATIONS

7.1 DISPLAYING INFORMATION IN COLUMNS

To display columns of information on a page with equal margins top and bottom and each side of the page when using a typewriter:

1. Clear margins and tabs.
2. Measure the paper and find the middle of its width.
3. Move the typing point to the middle of the width of the paper.
4. Find the longest line in each column in the table. In Example 3 the longest lines are:
   1st column: Czechoslovakia
   2nd column: Malaysia
   3rd column: New Zealand
   4th column: Sierra Leone.
5. Back-space once for every 2 letters and spaces in the longest line in each column and the spaces between the columns. You are advised to leave 3 spaces although any consistent number (more than 2 or 3 depending on the examining authority) is acceptable. In the example given you should back-space: Cz ec ho sl ov ak ia spacespace spaceM al ay si aspace spacespace Ne wspace Ze al an dspace space-space Si er ra spaceL eo ne. Had there been an odd letter you would have ignored it.
6. Set a margin at this point. (You could set a tab at this point but you would then have to return the carriage and press the tabulator to find this point for each line.)
7. Tap once on the space bar for each letter and space in the longest line in each column and the spaces between, setting a tab at the start of each column. For Example 3 tap:
   Czechoslovakia space space space – set a tab.
   Malaysia space space space – set a tab.
   New Zealand space space space – set a tab.

There is no point in tapping out the last column because you only need to know the starting point of it.

8. Measure the paper to find the middle of its depth. Put it into the machine at 0 on the scale on the left or balance it about 0 in the centre of the bail bar – depending on your machine. Line up the mid-point on the card holder.

9. Turn the roller towards you anticlockwise as though winding the paper back out of the machine, one 'click' for every line down the tabulation. (See also page 86.)

10. For the example given you will click:
1 (Belgium); 2 (Bermuda); 3 (Brazil); 4 (Burma); 5 (China); 6 (Cyprus); 7 (Czechoslovakia). Push the carriage back to the left margin (manual machines) or move the printing head to the left margin without turning up the paper (electric and electronic machines). This is the point at which you will start typing the tabulation.

If you are using a word processor you must follow the instructions given in the manual – these vary from machine to machine and program to program.

Example 3

Display the tabulation below on a sheet of A5 (210 × 148 mm) paper with equal margins top and bottom and on each side of the page. Follow the instructions already given and those given below the table.

Belgium	Denmark	Mexico	Sierra Leone
Bermuda	Ecuador	New Zealand	Singapore
Brazil	Ghana	Nigeria	Spain
Burma	Jamaica	Pakistan	Sudan
China	Kenya	Peru	Uganda
Cyprus	India	Poland	Venezuela
Czechoslovakia	Malaysia	Portugal	Yugoslavia

To type the tabulation

Type 'Belgium'. Press the tabulator to find the starting point of the second column. Type 'Denmark'. Press the tabulator to find the starting point of the third column. Type 'Mexico'. Press the tabulator to find the starting point of the fourth column. Type 'Sierra Leone'. Return the carriage and continue. *Always work across a tabulation and never down each column individually.*

Some electronic typewriters can set out column work automatically, as can word processors. Follow the instructions given in your machine manual as they vary from machine to machine.

Alternative method of calculating top and bottom margins

1. Find how many lines of type there are available down the page.
2. Calculate how many lines of type the tabulation will occupy.
3. Take the number of lines to be occupied by the table from the number of lines available down the page.
4. Divide the answer by 2 and add on 1. If there is a remainder, ignore it.
5. Put the paper into the machine and turn up the number of single line spaces calculated and type the table.

In the example on the previous page

1. There are 35 lines of type available on the page (A5–210 × 148 mm).
2. The tabulation occupies 7 lines.
3. 35 – 7 = 28.
4. 28 divided by 2 = 14. 14 + 1 = 15
5. Put the paper into the machine and turn up 15 single lines to type the tabulation.

Exercise 51

Display each table on a suitable sheet of paper with equal margins top and
bottom and at each side of the sheet.

Chicken	Grouse	Pigeon	Wild goose
Duck	Mallard	Quail	Moorhen
Goose	Partridge	Snipe	Woodcock
Turkey	Pheasant	Teal	Guinea fowl

asparagus	cabbages	cucumbers	mushrooms
aubergines	carrots	French beans	okra
avocado pears	cauliflowers	garlic	onions
beetroot	celery	globe artichokes	peppers
broad beans	chicory	lettuces	tomatoes
broccoli	courgettes	mange-tout peas	watercress

adding machine	coffee machine	drawing pin
addressing machine	computer desk	filing cupboard
anglepoise light	concertina file	insulated fire safe
answering machine	counter board	location panel
book rack	date stamp	masking tape
card index cabinet	digital calculator	notice board

full stop (period)	ellipses	parentheses
question mark	comma	brackets
exclamation mark	colon	hyphen
apostrophe	semi-colon	---
quotation mark	dash	---

aluminium	Al	cadmium	Cd	gold	Au
antimony	Sb	caesium	Cs	helium	He
argon	Ar	calcium	Ca	hydrogen	H
arsenic	As	carbon	C	iodine	I
barium	Ba	chlorine	Cl	iron	Fe
beryllium	Be	chromium	Cr	krypton	Kr
bismuth	Bi	cobalt	Co	lead	Pb
boron	B	copper	Cu	lithium	Li
bromine	Br	fluorine	F	magnesium	Mg

7.2 MAIN HEADINGS TYPED OVER TABULATIONS

Main headings over tabulations may be blocked at the left margin or they may be centred over the table. You should leave 2 blank lines (turn up 3 single lines) after a main heading although some authorities will accept one blank line left after a main heading (turn up 2 single lines).

Example 4
Type the tabulation below. Type the heading at the left margin. Use a suitable sheet of paper and centre the tabulation on the page with equal margins top and bottom and on each side.

STUDENTS ON COURSE 509

ABLEY Anne	EDWARDS Cyril	JORDAN Keith
ANSLOW David	FEENEY Kathleen	LOWE Elizabeth
BAKER Susan	GREY Arthur	MASOOD Ghashghai
CHILTON Alison	HAZELWOOD Andrew	O'ROURKE Ida
DALTON James	HOPLEY Doreen	PARKES Harry
DAMJI John	JEAVONS Timothy	WELSH Ian

Example 5
Type the tabulation below on a suitable sheet of paper with equal margins at top and bottom and on each side. Centre the main heading.

CAPITAL CITIES

Buenos Aires	Peking	Bonn	Nairobi
Canberra	Nicosia	Accra	Beirut
Vienna	Prague	Athens	Kuala Lumpur
Nassau	Copenhagen	New Delhi	Mexico City
Brussels	Quito	Tehran	The Hague
Hamilton	Cairo	Bagdad	Wellington
Brazilia	Addis Ababa	Jerusalem	Lagos
Rangoon	Helsinki	Rome	Oslo
Ottawa	Paris	Kingston	Karachi
Santiago	Bathurst	Tokyo	Singapore City

7.3 SUB-HEADINGS

Sub-headings should be typed in the same position as the main heading. If the main heading is typed at the left margin, the sub-heading should also be typed at the margin; if the main heading is centred, the sub-heading should also be centred. Leave *one* blank line between a main heading and a sub-heading (turn up 2 single lines). Leave 2 blank lines after a sub-heading and before the tabulation which follows. If a sub-heading is typed on more than one line it may be typed in single or double line spacing. A main heading is usually typed in capitals with or without underscore, while a sub-heading is usually typed with initial capitals and it is underscored.

Example 6
Display the tabulation below on a suitable sheet of paper with equal margins at top and bottom and on each side using the blocked style. Note the main and sub-headings.

MAIN AGENTS

Central Region Only

Acif Ltd	Breyer Ltd	Kehar Singh & Co
Adforce Plc	Dhiman & Sons	Keruf Ltd
Alan May Plc	Dow Internatinal Inc	McCrae's Pty
Alibhai & Co Ltd	Exim International	Mangal Singh & Sons
Bayusuf Bros	Harrtz & Bell Plc	O'Sullivan Pty
Behal & Co	K V Patel & Co	Westco Inc
Bhrat Pty	Karlsson & Co	Zurobi Ltd

Example 7
Display the tabulation below in the centred style on a suitable sheet of paper, with equal margins top and bottom and on each side of the page.

CAREERS SERVICE

Available Leaflets

Agriculture	Computer Work	Hairdressing
Armed Forces	Construction	Horticulture
Banking	Electrical Supply	Health Services
Catering	Forestry	Insurance
Civil Service	Fire Service	Jewellery
Communications	Gas Industry	Secretarial

7.4 COLUMN HEADINGS – BLOCKED STYLE

If the main and sub-headings are typed at the left margin the column headings should be typed at the left margin and at tab stops. Leave a blank line between the main and sub-headings. Leave 2 blank lines between the sub-heading and the column headings – if there is no sub-heading leave 2 blank lines between the main heading and the column headings. Leave one blank line between the column headings and the columns which follow. If a column heading has to be typed on more than one line type it in single line spacing.

Example 8

Display the following on a suitable sheet of paper with equal margins top and bottom and at each side of the page.

COVERALL PAINTS

Seasonal Range – Names and Code Numbers

Spring Time Green Range		Summer Heat Red Range		Autumn Hues Yellow Range	
Aquatine	201	Bandbox	301	Amberglow	401
Atlantis	202	Begonia	302	Bronze	405
Bangkok	203	Bolero	304	Corndolly	409
Bittersweet	205	Brigand	310	Copperglow	411
Crest	210	Cancan	315	Gazelle	412
Cucumber	211	Calypso	320	Gingernut	415
Eden	215	Dazzle	323	Harvestime	420
Figleaf	219	Flamingo	325	Maize	430
Grass	220	Heatwave	330	Mango	435
Lovage	225	Pimpernel	332	Nutmeg	445
Quince	230	Poppy	340	Strawtime	450
Spearmint	235	Scarlet	343	Tortoise-shell	460
Springtide	240	Sunset	345	Wheaten	466
Tumbleweed	245	Tangerine	350	Whispers	467

7.5 COLUMN HEADINGS – CENTRED STYLE

If the main and sub-headings are centred over the tabulation, the column headings should be centred over the columns. If a column heading is shorter than the column beneath it, it should be centred over the column. If the column heading is wider than the column beneath it, the column should be centred under the column heading.

Example 9

<u>UNIVERSAL 727 COMPUTER</u>

<u>Sample Software Packages</u>

<u>Business Applications</u>	<u>Games</u>	<u>General/Home Applications</u>
Accounting	Car Chase	Bank Statement
Cashbook	Chess	Budgeting
Communications	Darts	Call Account
Filing	Draughts	Car Maintenance
Job-costing	Dodgems	Diary
Mail Order	Ghosts	Freezer List
Hotel Guest	The Maze	Recipes
Word Processing	Star Wars	Shopping List

To type the above tabulation

1. Back-space the longest line in each column, once for every 2 letters and spaces plus 3 spaces between each column: 'Business Applications' and 3 spaces, 'Car Chase' and 3 spaces; 'General/Home Applications'. Set the left-hand margin and tabs as usual.
2. Click back to find the starting point or use the calculation method outlined on page 95.
3. Centre the main and sub-headings. Turn up 3 single lines (to leave 2 blank lines between the sub-heading and the column headings).
4. The longest line in the first column is the heading – type it at the left margin.
5. Press the tab to find the starting point of the second column. The heading is shorter than the longest line in the column 'Car Chase' so it must be centred over the column. To do this:
   (a) Tap once on the space bar for every 2 letters and spaces in the longest line in the column (to find the middle of the column): <u>Ca</u> <u>rspace</u> <u>Ch</u> <u>as</u> – ignore the odd letter 'e'.
   (b) Back-space the heading – once for every 2 letters (and spaces, if any). Back-space: <u>Ga</u> <u>me</u> – ignore the odd letter 's'. Type the heading 'Games'.

6. Press the tab and move to the start of the third column. The heading is the longest line, so type it.
7. Return the carriage twice to leave the required blank line after the column headings.
8. The column has to be centred under the heading. To do this find the middle of the heading and back-space, once for every 2 letters and spaces, the longest line in the column under the heading: Tap: Bu si ne ss spaceA pp li ca ti on (ignore the odd letter 's') to find the middle of the column. Back-space: Wo rd spaceP ro ce ss in (ignore the odd letter 'g'). All lines under the heading start at this point (you may want to set an extra tab at this point to save time). Type 'Accounting'.
9. Press the tab to find the starting point of the second column. All the items in the column start at this point, so type 'Car Chase'.
10. Press the tab to find the starting point of the third column. The items in the column have to be centred under the heading. Tap: Ge ne ra 1/ Ho me spaceA pp li ca ti on - ignore the odd letter 's'. Back-space: Ca rspace Ma in te na nc - ignore the odd letter 'e'. All the items in the column start at this point and you may want to set an extra tab here to save time later. Type 'Bank Statement'.
11. Return the carriage and finish the tabulation.

Type the tabulation on the previous page following the instructions given before attempting the one below. Use suitable sheets of paper for each and leave equal margins top and bottom and on each side of the page.

Example 10

F A B R I C S

New Seasons Ranges

Cotton	Cotton and Nylon Mix	Woollen Mixture
After eight	African	Australian
Bright lights	Asian	Charcoal
Casual	Atlantic	Knitting
Fashion free	European	Natural
Flower patterns	Indian	Shetland
Sports wear	Oriental	Spanish
Summer days	Pacific	Suiting

Exercise 52

Type the table on a suitable sheet of paper with equal margins top and bottom and at each side of the sheet. Use the blocked or the centred style – consistently.

Commercial Studies
Revision Check List

Methods of Payment	Ownership	Insurance
Bank Bills	Articles of Association	Actuary
Bank Notes	Authorised Capital	Annuity
Banker's Order	Called-up Capital	Assessor
Cheque	Certificate of Incorporation	Average Adjuster
Credit Transfer	Dividend	Certificate of Insurance
Currency	Issued Capital	Cover note
Direct Debit	Limited Liability	Endowment Assurance
Drawee	Memorandum of Association	Indemnity
Drawer	Nationalisation	Marine
Money order	Partnership	Mutual Life
Payee	Shares	Policy
Postal Order	Sole Trader	Premium
Standing Order	Prospectus	Proposal Form

Exercise 53

Type the tabulation on a suitable sheet of paper in the blocked *or* the centred style – consistently.

REFILL PADS

Student Range by Supreme

Reference Number	Size	Rulings Available	Number of Pages	Colour
F 203	330 × 203 mm	Feint	75	Yellow
FM 210	330 × 203 mm	Feint and Margin	80	Blue
NF 215	330 × 203 mm	Narrow Feint	80	Ochre
NFM 220	330 × 203 mm	Narrow Feint and Margin	80	Green
P300	210 × 297 mm	Plain	75	Red
F 305	210 × 297 mm	Feint	80	Yellow
FM312	210 × 297 mm	Feint and Margin	80	Blue
NF 320	210 × 297 mm	Narrow Feint	80	Ochre
NFM 330	210 × 297 mm	Narrow Feint and Margin	80	Green
G 340	210 × 294 mm	Graph	100	Orange
MP 350	210 × 297 mm	Music Pad 12 stave	100	Mauve

7.6 TABULATIONS WITH HORIZONTAL LINES

Tabulations with horizontal lines may be typed in the blocked or the centred style.

Example 11

CONTINENTAL AIRWAYS
_____

_____

CHARTER DESTINATIONS

_____

Agadir	Heraklion	Pula
Alicante	Ibiza	Reus
Almeria	Larnaca	Rhodes
Athens	Mahon	Tangeria
Barcelona	Malta	Thessalonika
Funchal	Naples	Tunis
Gerona	Palermo	Verona

_____

To type the above tabulation

1. Back-space the longest line in each column as usual to set the left margin.
2. Tap out the longest line in the first column and the 3 spaces after it to set the first tab. Tap: 'Barcelona' and 3 spaces.
3. Tap out the longest line in the second column and the 3 spaces after it to set the second tab. Tap: 'Heraklion' and 3 spaces.
4. Tap out the longest line in the third column and set a tab on *the last but one letter*. Tap: 'Thessalonik' – and set the tab on the 'k'.
5. Mark the mid-point of the paper and put it into the machine – or use the calculation method to determine how many lines to turn up. If you click back, click:
   1 (*CONTINENTAL AIRWAYS*); 2 (blank line); 3 (blank line); 4 (horizontal line); 5 (space after the horizontal line); 6 (CHARTER DESTINATIONS); 7 (horizontal line); 8 (space after the horizontal line); 9 (Agadir); 10 (Alicante); 11 (Almeria); 12 (Athens); 13 (Barcelona); 14 (Funchal); 15 (Gerona); 16 (horizontal line).
6. Type the heading and turn up to leave the required 2 blank lines.
7. Type one underscore at the left margin and at each of the tabs. This

will show you the length of the first horizontal line. You can either link your points with a line of underscores or you can use a pen with *matching ink* and a ruler to link them when you have finished the table.

8. Turn up 2 single lines and type 'CHARTER DESTINATIONS'.
9. Return the carriage and mark the left margin and tab points again using the underscore as before.
10. Turn up 2 single lines and type 'Agadir'.
11. Press the tab to find the second column and type 'Heraklion'.
12. Press the tab to find the third column and type 'Pula'.
13. Continue working through the tabulation. When you have typed 'Verona' return the carriage and use the underscore to mark the left margin and tab points as before.

POINTS TO REMEMBER

(i) Set the last tab on the *last but one* letter/character in the column on the right.
(ii) When counting the number of lines the tabulation occupies down the page – or when clicking back – count:
   (a) one for each horizontal (ruled) line;
   (b) one for the space *after* each horizontal (ruled) line.
   Do not count a space *before* a horizontal line within a tabulation.
(iii) When typing tabulations with horizontal lines turn up *2 single lines* after a horizontal line but only *one single line* before a horizontal line within a tabulation.

If you are using a word processor you should follow the instructions in the manual.

Type Examples 11 and 12 on suitably sized sheets of paper.

Example 12

CITY CARS — COLOURS AND TRIMS

All ranges

Exterior Colour	Interior Trims		
	Saloon	Coupe	Estate
Polar White	Red	Red	Red
Cinnabar Red	Blue	Blue	Blue
Henna Red	Red	Red	Red
Regal Red	Beige	Beige	Beige
Opaline Green	Beige	Green	Green
Reed Green	Black	Caviar	Caviar
Light Grey	Grey	Grey	Caviar
Dove Blue	Grey	Grey	Grey
Silver Leaf	Beige	Green	Grey
Black	Red	Red	Red

Exercise 54

Type the tabulation on a suitable sheet of paper in the blocked *or* the centred style. Use the underscore to rule the horizontal lines, or mark them and rule them later using matching ink and a ruler.

COMPUTER GUIDE
Selected items only

Model	Type	Language Included	Languages Available	Terb Format	Colours Available
Ace	8 bit	Basic	Pascal, Fortran	80 x 24	16
Basic	16 bit	None	Cobol, Basic	80 x 24	12
Capitol 820	8 bit	Basic	Pascal	40 x 25	1
Campus	16 bit	None	Most	80 x 25	16
DC Speedy	8 bit	Basic	None	40 x 24	1
Excell	16 bit	Basic	Pascal, CP/M	80 x 24	1
Micro ZP	8 bit	None	Any with CP/M	80 x 25	16
Super M	8 bit	Basic	Pascal	48 x 95	1
				80 x 25	1

Exercise 55

Type the tabulation on a suitable sheet of paper in the blocked *or* the centred style. Use the underscore to rule the horizontal lines or mark them and rule later using matching ink and a ruler.

LENS TEST
Medium Price Range

	Chindit	Excellent	Mint	Practical
Focal Length Range:	60-250mm	70-210mm	80-200mm	70-150mm
Aperture Range:	f4-f22	f2.8-f22	f3.5-f22	f1.8-f22
Zooming Action:	one touch	one touch	one touch	one touch
Closest Focusing:	0.5m	0.55m	0.65m	0.55m
Weight:	800g	750g	690g	790g
Filter Size:	62mm	50mm	65mm	52mm

7.7 DISPLAYED MATERIAL WITH A JUSTIFIED RIGHT-HAND MARGIN

To display material with a justified right-hand margin, set a right-hand margin in the position required and back-space each line, one back-space for each letter and space in each line so that when typed each line ends on the margin. Some electronic typewriters and word processors will do this automatically if you follow the manual instructions.

Display each of the following examples with a justified right-hand margin, leaving space on the left of them for the later insertion of a drawing not less than 38 mm (1½ in) wide. Use sheets of A6 paper (148 × 105 mm).

Example 13

```
              OLD STUDENTS' ASSOCIATION

                 ANNUAL DINNER DANCE

                                 at

                  The Airport Hotel

                on Friday 16 December

           7.30 for 8.00 pm until 1 am

         Dress Informal    Bar extension
```

Example 14

```
                 PARKFIELDS SCHOOL

           PARENT TEACHER ASSOCIATION

                        announce an

                 AFRO-ASIAN EVENING

         to be held in the School Hall

        on Wednesday 8 June at 2000 hrs

                             B A R

           Proceeds to the Building Fund
```

7.8 DISPLAYED MATERIAL WITH JUSTIFIED LEFT AND RIGHT MARGINS

To display material with justified left and right margins:

1. Clear margins and tabs. Measure the paper to find the middle of the width. From the mid-point, back-space once for every 2 letters and spaces in the longest line in each column and the spaces to be left between them. You are advised to leave 3 spaces between each column.
2. Set a left margin at the point reached.
3. Tap out the longest line in the column on the left, one tap for each letter and space, the spaces between the columns and the longest column on the right. Set a right margin (or tab) at the point reached.
4. All items in the left column start at the left margin. All items in the right column are back-spaced, one back-space for each letter and space in each line, so that when typed they all end flush on the right margin.

In Example 15:

1. Back-space Ed it or ia lspace Of fi ce rspace spacespace Ch ri st op he rspace Ch ie. Set a *left* margin.
2. Tap: Editorial Officer space space space Christopher Chie – and set a *right* margin or tab.

Users of word processors should follow the manual instructions.

Example 15
Display the following on a suitable sheet of paper with justified left and right margins.

CHARACTERS

in order of appearance

General Manager	Joseph Adetutu
Cashier	Helen Atkinson
News Editor	Christopher Chie
Secretary	Susan LLoyd
Editorial Officer	Alexander Cook
Foreman	David Osobase
First Worker	Robert Laughton
Second Worker	Christine Kidd

Exercise 56

Display the list on a suitable sheet of paper with justified left and right margins. Use equal margins top and bottom and at each side.

PRIZE WINNERS
(last year)

College of Higher Education

English Literature	Bridget D'Souza
Scientist of the Year	Gregory Bryan
Secretarial Cup	Elizabeth Hallett
Nursing Award	Rosalind Powell
Electronics Prize	George Wade
Business Studies Award	John Iwanowski
Design Award	Emile Alegria
Student of the Year	Harold Fernandez
Community Award	Grace Martin
Sports Person Cup	Pamela Scott
Mechanic of the Year	Ernest Woodward
Handicapped Student Cup	Nara Harragin
Horticulturalist Award	Karl Rzepka

Presentation by
Dr and Mrs David Noble FRCS

Exercise 57

Display the programme on a suitable sheet of paper with justified left and right margins.

ANNUAL CONFERENCE
PROGRAMME

<u>Friday</u>

1600 hrs onwards		Registration
2030 hrs	Opening of Conference by Chairman: Richard Gethin	
2045 hrs	From Scribes to Computers Speaker: John Rowland	

<u>Saturday</u>

0800 - 0900hrs		Breakfast
0930 hrs	Information Technology For All Speaker: Miss Mary Oldfield	
1030 hrs		Coffee
1100 hrs	Communications of the Future Speaker: Dr Mark Braun	
1245 - 1345 hrs		Lunch
1430 hrs	Annual General Meeting	
1500 hrs		Tea
2030 hrs	The Impact of the Laser Speaker: Dr Jacob Mathai	

<u>Sunday</u>

0800 - 0900 hrs		Breakfast
0930 hrs	The Future of Television Speaker: Ivan Butler	
1030 hrs		Coffee
1100 hrs	Closure of Conference by the new Chairman	
1215 hrs		Lunch

7.9 UNTOTALLED COLUMNS OF FIGURES

When figures are typed in untotalled columns they may be consistently aligned either on the left or on the right.

Type Examples 16 and 17 on suitable sheets of paper with equal margins top and bottom and on each side of the page.

Example 16
Aligned on the left

POPULATION FROM OVERSEAS

Country	Number	Country	Number
Austria	1 850 500	Jamaica	34 450
China	2 201 400	Japan	350 700
Czechoslovakia	502 000	Mexico	1 500 000
England	750 000	Philippines	78 500
Eire	867 000	Yugoslavia	34 500

Example 17
Aligned on the right

EXTERNAL TRADE

Country	Imports From	Exports To
United Kingdom	850 000 000	500 500 000
Canada	200 500 000	60 250 500
India	40 250 000	50 500 100
Pakistan	10 350 500	4 250 000
Malaysia	30 450 450	75 450 500
Japan	789 570 500	890 500 400
Saudi Arabia	45 900 000	7 590 000

FIGURES IN COLUMNS
WHICH ARE TOTALLED

Figures which are in columns to be totalled must be aligned on the right so that units align with units and so on. If the figures contain decimal points, these should be aligned. Some electronic typewriters and word processors will automatically align figures on the right – see the machine manual. See page 243 for standard and open puncuation in figures.

8.1 TO PRODUCE FINAL TOTALS IN COLUMNS ON A TYPEWRITER

1. Back-space the longest line in the column after typing the last figure(s) in the column and type an underscored line the length of the longest line in the column.
2. Turn up 2 single lines. Type the total. If there is a symbol indicating the figures in the total, e.g. £ or $, the symbol is typed to the left of the total, outside the line typed above, with no space between the symbol and the figure it represents.
3. Return the carriage (and turn up a single line).
4. Type a second underscored line the length of the first line.
5. Use the ratchet release to turn up roughly 1 mm and type a second line close to the previous underscored line.

When using some electronic typewriters and word processors it is impractical to type the 2 final lines as described above. A line of 'equals' signs is the usual solution unless there is a special head available.

Example 18
Type the columns below on a sheet of A5 (210 x 148 mm) paper with tabs
at *pica*: 25, 41 and 57; *elite*: 30, 50 and 70; *15 pitch*: 42, 62 and 82.

56.50	75.25	135.00
7.75	230.50	12 900.80
590.25	6.45	1 505.75
88.60	490.00	20 900.00
1.50	100.75	80 850.00
£744.60	£902.95	$116 291.55

Note the underscored lines are the length of the longest line in each
column – not necessarily the figure immediately above the first line.
Symbols representing the final totals are typed outside the underscored
lines.

8.2 TOTALLING COLUMNS OF FIGURES – ALTERNATIVE METHODS

While the method outlined above is the most universally acceptable one
for totalling columns of figures 3 other methods are also acceptable to
most examining authorities. These are:

Method 1 – leaving one blank line before typing the underscored line and a
blank line on both sides of the total. To do this:
1. Type the last amount in the column and return the carriage – turning
up a single line space as you do so.
2. Type the underscored line the length of the longest line in the column.
3. Return the carriage twice and type the final total.
4. Return the carriage once and type the 2 final lines as previously described.

Method 2 – as for the method outlined in section 8.1, but leaving half a
line space on both sides of the total. To do this:
1. Underscore the final figure in the column without turning up.
2. Turn up 1½ lines and type the final total.
3. Turn up half a line space to type the final 2 lines.

Method 3 – leaving half a line space before the first underscored line and
half a line space on both sides of the final total. To do this:
1. Turn up half a line space after the last item in the column and type the
underscored line as previously described.

2. Turn up 1½ lines and type the final total.
3. Turn up half a line space to type the final 2 lines as previously described.

Exercise 58

Type the columns, using any of the styles outlined, on a suitable sheet of paper.

2.50	35.50	126.00	12	250.50
110·75	1.75	65.28	1	200.75
5.25	96.72	297.74		975.00
26.38	46.29	170.76	2	125.50
18.46	102.31	86.00	4	500.00
37.00	4.90	125.90		250.50
$200.34	$287.47	£871.68	£21	302.25

8.3 FIGURES IN COLUMNS – POSITION OF THE UNIT AT THE HEAD OF THE COLUMN

The position of the unit of currency at the head of the column depends on the style being used.

Blocked style

When using the blocked style the unit of currency may be typed over the left of the column (Example 19) or over the units figure of the whole unit of currency (Example 20). Type the examples on a suitable sheet of paper.

Example 19	Example 20

£	$
50.00	300.00
5.00	56.50
10.75	24.50
£65.75	$381.00

Centred style

When typing whole numbers only the unit of currency may be typed over the middle figure (Example 21), while if the column contains decimal units as well as whole numbers the unit of currency must be typed over the unit figure of the whole units (Example 22). Type the examples on a suitable sheet of paper.

Example 21	Example 22

```
        £                    $
   10 340                  5.75
    1 500                 75.45
   25 360                112.34
   ───────               ──────
   £37 200              $193.54
   ═══════              ══════
```

It can be seen from the above that Examples 20 and 22 are acceptable no matter what style is used.

8.4 UNTOTALLED COLUMNS

If columns are untotalled the unit of currency may be typed before each sum rather than at the head of the column, which can be aligned on the left or the right depending on the style of the rest of the work, for example:

Aligned right   *Aligned left*

```
   £35.00            $45.98
  £234.50            $456.70
   £5.00             $5.50
```

8.5 TYPING DECIMAL PARTS OF WHOLE UNITS OF CURRENCY IN TOTALLED COLUMNS

When typing such units as pence (p) and cents (c) at the head of columns containing these units, only the unit figure may be typed on the left (Examples 23 and 24) or on the right (Examples 25 and 26). Type the examples on a suitable sheet of paper.

Example 23	Example 24	Example 25	Example 26
p	c	p	c
10	12	15	20
6	9	11	34
61	22	16	21
77	43	42	75

Some authorities require a '0' entered in the tens figure of a column where there are units of figures only, e.g. 06, 09.

8.6 UNTOTALLED COLUMNS OF DECIMAL UNITS OF CURRENCY

Untotalled columns of decimal units of currency may be aligned on the left or the right – depending on the style of the rest of the work. The unit of currency follows the figures, for example:

Aligned right   *Aligned left*

23c	75p
5c	9p
90c	45p

8.7 PUNCTUATION OF MONEY AND UNITS OF MEASUREMENT IN COLUMNS

When typing sums of money and units of measurement in totalled or untotalled columns, standard or open punctuation may be used provided the use is consistent. See Appendix C.

Exercise 59

Practise typing sums of money in columns. Use any consistent style and a suitable sheet of paper.

£	£	$	$	$
297.25	16.87	40.30	29.60	1.00
25.75	17.87	14.70	11.40	16.00
31.60	9.45	18.95	2.40	6.30
8.27	4.50	16.27	81.26	40.82
27.80	18.40	22.50	21.77	55.81
132.77	95.20	44.90	26.30	84.20
16.31	29.40	81.20	92.40	7.25
£ 539.75	£ 191.69	$238.82	$265.13	$211.38

Exercise 60

Type the sums of money in columns using any consistent style and a suitable sheet of paper.

£	£	$	$
12,200	139	450	610
8,250	436	102	94
56	8	5	210
1,266	27	48	18
16,754	222	4	9
£ 38,526	£ 832	$ 609	$ 941

Exercise 61

Type the units of measurement in columns using any consistent style and a suitable sheet of paper.

km	km	m	cm
21 400.5	108.66	4.26	1.25
8 552.6	96.30	9.42	18.65
227.0	425.90	18.76	4.80
30 180.1	630.86	32.44	24.70

LEADER DOTS

Leader dots are used to lead the eye from one column to another. They may be produced in 4 different ways, though only one style should be used in a particular piece of work.

9.1 CONTINUOUS DOTS

Much the easiest method to produce. Leave a space before the first dot on the left and ensure that all dots end at the same place on the right. To do this go to the start of the right-hand column and back-space twice. Set a tab. This is the position of the last dot in the row.

Example 27
Type the following on a suitable sheet of paper and insert continuous leader dots. Leave any convenient number of spaces between the columns.

CHARACTERS IN ORDER OF APPEARANCE

```
Andrew James ........ Ernest Woodward
Monica Miller ....... Sheila Thompson
Reginald Metzger .... Bert Phillips
Patrick Muruatetu ... Dennis Richards
Jim Stewart ......... James Gwilt
Mary Grafton ........ Barbara Harrison
Grant Alexander ..... Ronald Tromans
Mary McDougall ...... Sally Hawkins
Peter Williams ...... Anthony Rey
```

9.2 ONE DOT AND THREE SPACES

Some authorities prefer 1 dot and 4 spaces but 1 dot and 3 spaces is universally acceptable. To produce this group on a typewriter:

1. Set a tab for the start of the *longest* item in the column on the right.
2. Back-space 4 spaces from that point. Set a tab. Continue back-spacing and setting a tab at every fourth back-space until you reach the *shortest* column on the left.
3. Type one dot at each tab having ensured that there is *at least one space* before the first dot on the left.

Example 28
Type the index which follows on a suitable sheet of paper using the one dot and 3 spaces methods outlined above.

```
INDEX


From the Editor    .   .   .   .   .   .   .        5
New Cars and Trucks    .   .   .   .   .   .        9
Readers' Letters .   .   .   .   .   .   .         71
Reference Section:
    New Cars    .   .   .   .   .   .   .   .       78
    New Trucks .   .   .   .   .   .   .   .      102
    Used Cars  .   .   .   .   .   .   .   .      130
    Used Trucks    .   .   .   .   .   .   .      156
Finance  .   .   .   .   .   .   .   .   .        165
Equipment Preview   .   .   .   .   .   .         176
Legal Department .   .   .   .   .   .   .        197
Club News    .   .   .   .   .   .   .   .        208
```

In the above example note the use of the *inset section* which indicates subsections within a section.

9.3 TWO DOTS AND THREE SPACES

In this method, 2 full stops are typed at each tab setting and 3 spaces are left after each grouping. To produce this on a typewriter:

1. Set a tab for the start of the *longest* line in the column on the right.
2. Back-space 5 spaces from this point and set a tab. Continue back-spacing and setting a tab at every fifth back-space until you reach the *shortest* column on the left.

3. Type 2 full stops at each tab, having ensured that there is at least one space between the first pair of dots and the line on the left.

Example 29

Type the exercise on a suitable sheet of paper using the 2 dots and 3 spaces method. Leave any convenient number of spaces between the column on the left and the column on the right.

DISTANCE COVERED BY DRIVERS

```
John Walker-Munro      ..   ..   ..   ..    756.2
John Gould  ..   ..   ..   ..   ..   ..     781.3
Mervyn Cowie      ..   ..   ..   ..   ..     805.6
Mary Archer ..   ..   ..   ..   ..   ..     819.2
Hilda Burgess      ..   ..   ..   ..   ..    923.8
Kathleen Murphy ..   ..   ..   ..   ..     1045.6
```

9.4 THREE DOTS AND TWO SPACES

This method is the same as 2 dots and 3 spaces, except that 3 full stops are typed at each point instead of 2 - leaving 2 spaces and not 3.

Example 30

Type the example using 3 dots and 2 spaces on a suitable sheet of paper.

```
TOPIC                                SPEAKER

New taxation legislation      ...  John W Smith
Computer accounting      ...  ...  Roger Nelson
Stock control      ...  ...  ...  Nigel Lawson
Staff records      ...  ...  ...  Mark Tudor
Welfare ...  ...  ...  ...  ...  Dr Mary Bolton
Robots  ...  ...  ...  ...  ...  Henry Wilkinson
```

If you are using a word processor consult your manual for procedure.

REMEMBER: No matter what system of leader dots you decide to use, be consistent within a piece of work. Always leave a space before the first leader dot on the left and at least one space between the last leader dot on the right and the material which follows. No line of typing should extend beyond the leader dots. The leader dots must align with each other.

Exercise 62
Type the exercise below on a suitable sheet of paper using any consistent style of leader dots.

TELEPHONE NUMBERS

Head Office	..	..	..	..	..	..	..	313232
Central Region	..	..	..	..	..	..	..	721200
Eastern Region	..	..	..	..	..	..	..	502341
Northern Region	..	..	..	..	..	..	..	2971
Western Region	..	..	..	..	-	..	..	45450
Security	..	..	..	..	..	..	..	321775
Transport	..	..	..	..	..	..	..	45455
Training Office	..	..	..	..	..	..	..	2777

124

Exercise 63
Display this tabulation in the centre of a suitable sheet of paper and insert
leader dots using any consistent style.

TAKINGS BY SECTIONS
Figures in 000s

Section	This year	Last year
Confectionery	530.6	490.7
Drinks	326.4	316.8
Tea and Foods	296.2	287.4
Chemicals and Drugs	45.9	44.1
Totals	1199.1	1139.0

Exercise 64
Display this tabulation in the centre of a suitable sheet of paper and insert leader dots using any consistent style.

GEOGRAPHICAL ANALYSIS

__In millions__

Area	This Year	Last Year
United Kingdom	650·2	625·6
Africa	270·6	260·1
Asia	97·4	98·3
Europe	110·7	128·2
North America	90·2	87·3
South America	25·6	30·4
Rest of the World	26·2	17·1
Total	1270·9	1247·0

BOXED RULED TABULATIONS

10.1 BOXED RULED TABULATIONS – BLOCKED STYLE

Example 31

Make	Weeks delivery	Dealers
Alfa-Romeo	3-5	150
Audi	4-6	410
Datsun	1-3	560
Ford	0-6	1250
Mazda	0-4	216

To set the left margin and tabs for the above example:

1. Clear margins and tabs. Measure the paper and find the middle of its width. Move the typing point to that point.
2. Back-space once for every 2 lines, letters and spaces in the longest line in each column to set the left margin. *Note*: each vertical line (line running down the tabulation) counts as a space. Leave one space on both sides of a vertical line within a tabulation. (Any consistent number will do but the space line and space between columns within a tabulation equals the 3 spaces you have been advised to leave in other tabular material). In the above display the longest lines in each column are: 'Alfa-Romeo', 'Weeks delivery' and 'Dealers'.
3. Back-space: linespace Al fa –R om eo spaceline spaceW ee ks spaced el iv er yspace linespace De al er sspace – ignore the odd line. Set the left margin.

4. Tap *once* for *every* line, space and letter across the tabulation, setting tabs for the vertical lines. For the above example tap: (line) space (Alfa-Romeo) space. Set a tab. (Line) space (Weeks delivery) space. Set a tab. (Line) space (Dealers) space. Set a tab.

Remember, when you marked the horizontal lines you set the tab on the *last but one* letter/item in the column. This is exactly what has happened here – you set the tab on the space before the vertical line each time.

To calculate the top and bottom margins for this example:

1. Find the middle of the depth of the paper and insert it into the machine. Align it on the card-holder.
2. Click back one click for every line and space down the tabulation. Click: 1 (ruled line); 2 (space after the line); 3 (Make); 3 (ruled line); 5 (space after the line); 6 (Alfa-Romeo); 7 (Audi); 8 (Datsun); 9 (Ford); 10 (Mazda); 11 (ruled line).

To type the tabulation:

1. Mark the left margin and tab points with the underscore – with the machine on 'stencil' if you want to hide the points later.
2. Turn up 2 single lines to leave the required blank line after the first horizontal line.
3. From the left margin tap once for the vertical line and once for the space after it. Type 'Make'. Press the tab and find the first tab. Tap once for the vertical line and once for the space after it. Type 'Weeks delivery'. Repeat the process for the last column.
4. Return the carriage and mark the left margin and tab points with the underscore.
5. Turn up 2 single lines (to leave the required blank line after the horizontal line).
6. Tap once for the vertical line and once for the space after it. Type 'Alfa-Romeo'. Press the tab and go to the first tab. Tap once for the vertical line and once for the space after it. Type '3–5'. Continue and complete the rest of the tabulation.
7. After the last item '216' return the carriage and mark the left margin and tab points with the underscore.

10.2 **RULING UP**

Use a ruler and matching ink or ball-point pen (never pencil). Place the *bevelled* edge of the ruler on the display as you rule. Rule in the order shown below. Rule to the *outside* of the *outside* points first and rule to the *middle* of the *mid-points*. Rule the vertical lines before ruling the horizontal lines – otherwise you will cover the markers.

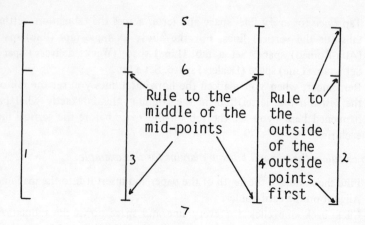

Rule to the middle of the mid-points

Rule to the outside of the outside points first

Rule the horizontal lines last to cover the underscore points

10.3 BOXED RULED TABULATIONS ON WORD PROCESSORS

Some electronic typewriters and word processors can rule up boxed ruled tabulations. The vertical lines are often ruled using a series of apostrophes in line while the horizontal lines are ruled using the underscore. Consult your manual for the capabilities of your particular machine. You may find that you can set out and print tabulations off the screen in a fashion very similar to that previously described for producing tabulations on a typewriter, for later ruling as described in section 10.2.

Exercise 65
Display the tabulations which follow on suitable sheets of paper and rule them up.

RANGE	COLOUR	CODE	WIDTH	PRICE
Thames	Yellow	40	1.0m	A
Nile	Red	50	1.5m	B
Darling	Green	60	2.0m	C
Indus	Blue	70	2.5m	D

Team	Played	Won	Drawn	Lost
Northfield	20	18	2	0
Capitol	20	15	1	4
Southern Ridge	20	14	2	4
Western Zone	20	13	2	5
Central City	20	10	4	6
Central District	20	9	4	7
Forresters	20	6	6	8
Rangers	20	6	5	9
South Bay	20	5	5	10
United	20	4	5	11
High Peak	20	3	1	16

Exercise 66
Display each tabulation on a suitable sheet of paper and rule up.

ELECTROLYSIS IN SOLUTIONS
Effects at cathode and anode

SOLUTION	ELECTRODE	CATHODE	ANODE
copper chloride	graphite	copper	chlorine
copper sulphate	copper	copper	anode dissolves
sodium hydroxide	platinum	hydrogen	oxygen
sulphuric acid	platinum	hydrogen	oxygen

ANALYSIS OF ENTRY
Summer Series only

Mode of Examination	Boys	Girls	Total
1	36 700	37 200	73 900
2	1 250	1 500	2 750
3	410	125	535
Total	38 360	38 825	77 185

10.4 BOXED RULED TABULATIONS – CENTRED STYLE

Example 32

Subject	Papers Worked	Passed	Failed
Audio–typewriting	40	31	9
Business Studies	58	42	16
Company Law	12	9	3
English Language	75	61	14

To type the above, centring the heading over the first column and the remaining columns under the other column headings:

1. Back-space from the centre of the page to set the left-hand margin and tab points as usual. Back-space: linespace Au di o - ty pe wr it in gspace linespace Pa pe rs spaceW or ke dspace linespace Pa ss ed spaceline spaceF ai le dspace – ignore the odd line. Set the margin. Tap out: line space Audio-typewriting space. Set a tab. Tap: line space Papers Worked space. Set a tab. Tap: line space Passed space. Set a tab. Tap: line space Failed space. Set a tab.
2. Click back from the centre of the depth of the page to find the starting point (or calculate and turn up).
3. Mark the left margin and tab points using the underscore. Turn up 2 single lines.
4. Centre 'Subject' over the first column. To do this, find the middle of the column by tapping once for every 2 lines, letters and spaces in the longest line in the column. Tap: linespace Au di o- ty pe wr it in gspace (the same as you back-spaced earlier). Back-space the heading: Su bj ec – ignore the odd letter 't'. Type 'Subject' in the centre of the column.
5. Press the tabulator to find the first tab. The heading is the longest line in the column, so tap: line space – and type 'Papers Worked'.
6. Press the tabulator and type the other column headings in the same way. Return the carriage and mark the margin and tab points with the underscore. Turn up 2 single lines.
7. From the margin, tap: line space – and type 'Audio-typewriting'. Press the tabulator to find the start of the second column.
8. Find the centre of the column. Tap: linespace Pa pe rs spaceW or ke dspace. Back-space once for every 2 figures in the longest

line in the column. Back-space 45 – and type '45' in the centre of the column.

9. Press the tabulator and repeat the process for the third column. Tap: linespace Pa ss ed spaceline – and back-space 31 then type '31' in the centre of the column.

10. Press the tabulator to find the starting point of the last column. Find the centre of the column. Tap: linespace Fa il ed spaceline. Back-space the longest line in the column – 14. This is the starting point of the longest line in the column but because you want to align the figures on the right you must tap in for the '1' to enable you to type 9 in the correct position.

Type example 32 on a sheet of A5 (210 × 148 mm) paper as indicated and rule up.

Electronic typewriters and word processors will often automatically centre material or align it correctly in columns – see the machine manual.

Exercise 67

Type the tabulation below on a suitable sheet of paper in the centred style and rule up.

DISTRICT AUTHORITY

Number of Employees

Department	Male	Female
Administration	136	227
Building Construction and Repairs	321	47
Education	650	776
Health/Social Services .	427	946
Road Construction and Repairs	172	26
Transport	92	47
Water	46	29
Other	94	107
TOTALS	1 938	2 205

10.5 **TABULATIONS WITH FOOTNOTES**

Footnotes add to the information given in a tabulation (see also page 184). Symbols or figures are used to differentiate between each footnote and what it means. In a table the footnote sign is typed directly after the item to which it refers with no space between it and the symbol used. Leave a blank line at the foot of the table before typing the footnote symbol at the left margin. Leave a space between the footnote symbol and the material which follows. Footnotes are typed in single line spacing with a blank line between items. The second or subsequent lines of footnotes may be aligned with the footnote symbol or the first word of the footnote. Some examination authorities accept footnotes centred under tables. If you are using a word processor check to see if your printer will print footnote symbols. Look in the manual under superscripts and strikeover for details of symbols and under print controls for details of printing capability.

Exercise 68
Type the tabulation with footnotes below on a suitable sheet of paper.

RECOMMENDED WINES

No order of preference implied

WHITE*		RED[‡]	
Sweet	Dry	Light	Full bodied
Ruster Ausbruch	Chenin Blanc	Pinot Noir	Barolo
Bordeaux	Traminer	Jura	Burgundy
Vouvray	Mosel	Chianti	Bordeaux
Riesling	Sauvignons	Demestica	St Julien
Passito	Steen	Petite Sirahs	Merlot
Muscat	Tokay	Gamay Noir	Crenache
Sauternes	Frascati	Cabernet	Beaujolais
Barsac	Sylvaner	Rioja	Margaux

* Serve slightly chilled

[‡] Serve at room temperature

Exercise 69
Display the following tables on suitable sheets of paper.

APPLICATIONS AND ADMISSIONS
FOR (LAST YEAR)

	Arts	Social Sciences	Technology/ Science	Mathematics	Total*
Applications	12,520	11,451	15,260	7,491	46,722
Admissions†	5,621	6,219	7,101	2,936	21,877

* This is the total number applying and admitted. Some students applied for, and were admitted to, more than one course.

† Of those admitted some 296 students left before the end of the year.

WORLD TEMPERATURES *

Town	Conditions†	°C	°F
Algiers	S	21	70
Bahrain	S	28	82
Barbados	F	29	84
Cairo	S	28	82
Geneva	R	11	52
Las Palmas	F	19	66
Los Angeles	F	19	66
Nairobi	F	27	81
Rio de Janeiro	C	26	79

* Noon   2 April

† S = sunny; F = fair; C = cloudy; R = rain

Exercise 70
Display the following tables on suitable sheets of paper and rule up.

AIRLINE SIZE COMPARISON

Name	No of aircraft *	Flights per week	City pairs served
Air America	31	2206	87
Austral/Pacific	29	2321	91
Continental	75	5102	140
Donnelly	60	2721	135
Euro/American	43	2496	91
Pan-African	32	2118	70

* Includes all types over 136 seaters

FUEL CONSUMPTION - OFFICIAL FIGURES*

Model	Urban Driving	Constant speed	
		90 km/h	120 km/h
Conurbation 1.1 2-door	8.6	6.2	8.8
Conurbation 1.3, 1.3L 2-door	9.1	6.1	8.7
Conurbation 1.3, 1.3L 4-door	9.1	6.1	8.7
Flier 1.1 2 and 4-door	10.1	6.9	8.5
Flier 1.3L and GS	10.8	6.9	8.4
Hi-Life 1.1 2-door	9.1	6.7	7.2
Hi-Life 1.3L and GS	9.0	6.9	9.4
Hi-Life 1.7L	10.9	8.2	11.0

* litres per 100 km

136

ANALYSIS OF QUALIFICATIONS

Job	Academic Qualifications			
	None	Elementary	Advanced	Degree
Chief	25	40	10	2
Laboratory Technician	2	5	26	4
Cashier	0	4	30	5
Nurse	0	10	38	5
Printer	10	37	7	1
Sales Representative	6	29	48	11
Courier	2	21	60	21

YOUNG OFFICE STAFF *

Sex	Categories		
	Machine † Operators	Clerks	Others
Male	1,216	3,426	902
Female	9,321	4,917	1,010
Total	10,537	8,343	1,912

* Under 21 years of age in all divisions
† Mainly microcomputers with range of programs

INCUBATION PERIODS

in days

Species	Shortest	Longest	Usual
Hen	20	22	21
Turkey	25	28	28
Duck	28	30	29
Goose	28	32	32
Pigeon	17	19	18

TRADE FIGURES - EXPORTS TO

1st Quarter - in 000s

Region	January	February	March
Australasia . . .	10.4	9.3	11.7
Canada	6.3	5.1	6.2
EEC	121.6	120.0	121.9
EFTA	86.3	77.2	87.0
Japan	2.3	1.7	3.8
Malaysia	9.3	8.0	10.4
Mexico	1.1	0.8	2.3
North Africa . .	38.4	35.7	39.0
South America .	10.2	8.3	11.4
Rest	22.6	25.4	23.1
TOTAL	308.5	291.5	316.8

Present Age	Net Monthly Investments of 10 units		
	Guaranteed Sum	Guaranteed Bonus	Projected Value
30	1250	662	1912
31	1250	662	1912
32	1249	660	1909
33	1248	659	1907
34	1247	658	1905
35	1245	657	1902
36	1244	656	1900
37	1244	655	1899
38	1243	654	1897
39	1242	653	1895
40	1241	651	1892

LOAN REPAYMENT TABLE
at 10% pa flat rate

Units Borrowed	12 Months			24 Months		
	Monthly Repayment	Total Interest	Total Repayment	Monthly Repayment	Total Interest	Total Repayment
10	0.92	1.00	11.00	0.50	2.00	12.00
50	4.59	6.00	55.00	2.50	10.00	60.00
100	9.17	10.00	110.00	5.00	20.00	120.00
500	45.84	50.00	550.00	25.00	100.00	600.00
1000	91.67	100.00	1100.00	50.00	200.00	1200.00

10.6 THE BRACE

The brace takes the place of the handwritten bracket which is sometimes used to connect two or more lines of type. The brackets (and) are used – depending on which way the brace is to face. They may be produced with no space between them and the longest line in the section, as in Example 33; with a space between them and the longest line in the section, as in Example 34; in a straight line connecting two or more sections with no space between them and the longest line, as in Example 35; or with one space between them and the longest line, as in Example 36. Be consistent in any piece of work and set an extra tab in whatever position you decide to type the brace.

Example 33

```
J Andrews    )
R Dawson     )
M Talibhusein)

J Urmson )
A Vickers)
```

Example 34

```
Mars    )
Jupiter )
Venus   )

Saturn )
Pluto  )
```

Example 35

```
Lead      )
Zinc      )
Tin       )

Copper   )
Aluminium)
```

Example 36

```
Opal     )
Diamond )
Topaz   )

Emerald )
Ruby    ) ⌐
```

Exercise 71

Practise the brace. Set out the following on a suitable sheet of paper.

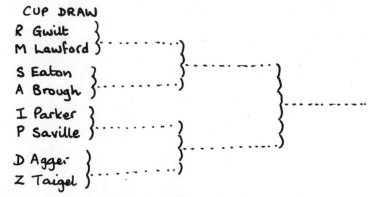

Exercise 72

Set out the following on a suitable sheet of paper.

ERAS	PERIODS
	(Quaternary (Pleistocene and Recent)
	(Pliocene)
Cainozoic	(Miocene) Tertiary
	(Oligocene)
	(Eocene)
	(Upper Cretaceous
	(Lower Cretaceous
Mesozoic	(Jurassic
	(Triassic
	(Permian
	(Carboniferous
	(Devonian
Palaeozoic	(Silurian (Upper Silurian)
	(Ordovician (Lower Silurian)
	(Cambrian
	(Torridonian
Pre-Cambrian	(Lewisian

Exercise 73
Set out the following on a suitable sheet of paper.

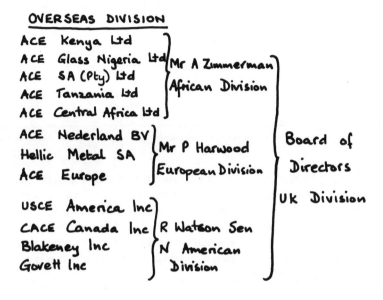

CHAPTER 11

CORRECTION SIGNS

Printers use a form of shorthand to indicate errors in setting material to be printed and these correction signs are widely used in offices to indicate errors in typed or printed material. You should get into the habit of using them to correct errors in your own work. The list below contains the most commonly used signs. A sign is usually made in the text at the point of the error to draw attention to it and, if required, further information is given in a sign or signs in either margin.

11.1 SIGNS IN THE TEXT

Sign	Meaning
/	Something is incorrect. See either margin for correction.
⋏	Something has been left out.
⌒	Close up a space.
⌒	Change round the order of the word or letters indicated.
⌐	Start a new paragraph.
⌒	Do not start a new paragraph - continue with the old one.
....	Leave in the word(s) - ignore the crossing out.

11.2 SIGNS IN THE MARGIN

Sign	Meaning
CAPS or u c	Change the letter(s) indicated to capital (upper case) letters.
Lc	Change the letter(s) indicated to small (lower case) letters.
#	Put in a space where indicated in the text.
close up	Close up a space where indicated in the text.

NPor PARA Start a new paragraph where indicated in the text.

ı–ı   Put in a hyphen.

ı—ı   Put in a dash.

trs   Change round the order of the words or letters indicated.

run on Do not start a new paragraph - continue with the old one.

stet   Let it stand - leave in the word(s) indicated by the dots.

⊙ ⊙   Put in a comma/full stop as indicated.

ʹ̓ ʺ̓   Put in single/double quotes as indicated.

ℒ   Leave out the word(s) indicated. The sign is made by joining the letters d e l (the first letters in the word 'delete') in one outline.

Two parallel lines running vertically down a margin indicate that the margin needs straightening.

In addition to using correction signs, *balloons* and *arrows* may be used to indicate the position of material. If you want to photocopy material which has been edited in such a way as not to show the editing on the photocopy you should use a light (Cambridge) blue pencil since this does not show on most photocopies.

Exercise 74

Take a corrected copy of the following exercise on paper of a suitable size.

<u>Climate</u> *caps*

```
                    Modern man is just as con̂cerned about the    [c above]
      ⊙/⊙    weather as his ancestors and⁄like them⁄ he
                    seeks to understand and predict it.  Ideally
                    he would like to control it but that time
      #/NP   would seem to be a long⁄way off. ⁄What man is
      ⍺            coming to believe is that the debris⁄ from
   e/stet   volcano⁄s thrown high into the atmospher⁄.
      ⌣           prevents the sun⁄s rays from reaching the
                    surface of the earth and from time to time
      s/⊙    cause⁄ the climate to cool slightly⁄
  run on
  stet       It is known that there have been ~~many~~ ice
                    ages and it is thought that they might have
      NP      been caused by such activity. ⁄Another claim
                    is that the burning of carbon fuels such as
                    coal and petrol will trap heat within the
                    atmosphere and prevent the natural cooling
  cause   of the earth - and⁄ temperatures to rise.
                       (and melt the polar ice)
```

Exercise 75

Produce a corrected copy of the following article on a suitable sheet of paper.

What's in a memory? *Caps and underscore*

= *Extra space here please*

Look up the word 'memory' in a dictionary and you will probably find
statements to the effect that memory is the mental capacity or faculty of
recalling previous experience or storing current experience for future use.
Microcomputer users are concerned with several kinds of memory in addition
to that bestowed upon them by nature (their own brain). The most commonly
used kinds of memory in computing are what are called rom and ram.

ROM is short for Read Only Memory and this is information stored in a 'chip'
— itself a shortened form of 'microchip'. A microchip is a circuit which
has been greatly reduced by various methods on to small pieces of silicon
or other material. A circuit is, in turn, a number of small electronic
components which have been linked together to form a particular function.
A microcomputer has a number of these, all performing special functions. A
chip which performs a read only function has been fed information which is
locked into it ready for reading by the user of the equipment. Perhaps most
forms of ROM are those in electronic watches and calculators. (*Common*)

RAM is short for Random Access Memory and this usually takes the form of
information held in a microcomputer in the form of electrical impulses ready
to be juggled about. Once the machine is switched off the memory vanishes (*usually*)
so if is wanted again it has to be stored on tape or disks.

Exercise 76

Copy the article below, using a suitable sheet of paper and making the required corrections.

INFORMATION STORAGE → *Centred over typing line. Please indent the paragraphs and change the paragraph headings to shoulder headings typed in capitals without underscore.*

1-1 *#*   Computers need a store of information if they are to work – they cannot work in a void. Some computers have a built/in store~in~the form of ROM and this~the information is stored on one or more chips. This store is captive – it is fixed into the machine. In order to be used for a range of ~tasks a computer *other* *usually* needs to be fed information and this is/done~by tape or disk. ~some~ *of information*

their   Tape. Any ordinary cassette ~tape~ *tape* deck can be plugged into ɑ computer/which s can then take information stored on~the tape into ~its~ RAM (Random Access *Memories* ~Memory~) where it can be handled in a variety of ways. The problem with this *close up* form of storage is the rate at which it can be fed into the computer memory. This feeding rate is described in terms of a measure~ment called Baud. The bigger the Baud figure the faster the rate of input. Another problem with this form of storage is that if the computer wants some information further along the tape it has to wait until all the information has been fed in. *be able to use a realistic*

k/s   Disk. To ~hold~ ~any~ ~viable~ quantity of information a computer needs one or *s* more disc/ drives. There are many forms of disk/but essentially they are *as* rather like a long-playing record/except that they can be fed information ɤ well as storing it. Any information already on a disk can be recorded over.

Exercise 77

Copy the following article on a suitable sheet of paper, making the required corrections.

Disk Storage – *Spaced caps and underscore*

= *Extra space here please*

1–1 Disks are produced in an ever increasing range of sizes and formats but

storage they have one thing in common – they are a ~~store~~ place for computer

information. *TYPIST! Please type this article in the blocked style. Change the*

shoulder headings to paragraph headings typed with an initial capital

FLOPPY DISKS *letter. Type a full stop after each paragraph heading. Type the*

article in double line spacing.

As their name suggests, these disks are very flexible and look rather

like the free advertising disks often given away for playing on an ordinary

record player. In order to protect them they are encased in a cardboard

sleeve so that they appear to be square. Floppy disks may be single or

double sided and they may be single or double density. A single density one

disk sided floppy will not store as much information as a double density double

sided disk. The type of disk used will be determined by the computer and

the disk drive. Unless the head in the drive can 'read' the information

from the disk the information is us~~e~~less – although most heads designed to

can

read infor~~a~~mtion from a single density disk ~~and~~ use a double density disk.

The usual sizes of disks are 5¼ or 8 inch although some memory

typewriters use a smaller size – the so-called 3½ inch micro-floppy.

HARD DISKS

Hard disks.

~~These~~ are rigid disks and they are usually made of aluminium. They

huge are capable of storing quantities of information and they are ~~very~~ expensive.

Exercise 78

Copy the article below on a suitable sheet of paper, making the required corrections.

W I N C H E S T E R S – Closed caps. Please copy using a 60 character line length and double line spacing.

Probably
trs/e/uc Ask the man in the street, "What is a Winchester?" and you will be told that
it is/was a famous rifle and that it was used by the heros of many westerns.
would An office worker or a computer user might tell you that it is a form of hard
NP disk. An even more informed person would be able to tell you that the system
was developed by IBM – International Business Machines. Winchesters store a
great deal more information than the conventional 'floppies' and because they
are sealed in an airtight casing they are dirt and dust free. This means
much that they last longer than conventional disks and they are more reliable. A
conventional disk drive read-write head has to be able to find the right
∂ track on a disk – a difficult enough task with conventional grooving. The
task is more difficult when the grooves are even closer together. IBM
developed a system which does away with the conventional read-write head and
e the whole unit is exchangable – the 'head' floats over the Winchester on a
cushion of air and further reduces wear. This cushion of air is as small as
NP twenty millionths of an inch. The idea is still being developed and firms
4/4 such as Seagate and Syquist may be the storage kings of the future. *name*
Winchesters are much more expensive than conventional storage disks but they
are more reliable and they can store a vast amount of data. The first
e/M Winchesters were 14 inches across but now they are 8 inches, 5¼ and 3¼ inches.

Exercise 79

Copy the following article using a suitable sheet of paper and making the required corrections.

A New measurements   Caps centred over typing line. Use double line spacing please.

Computer memories are measured in kbytes – a measurement unknown only just a few years ago. A Kbyte is a unit of 1024 characters and a character can be a letter, figure, symbol or a space. Given that 5 characters make a typing word it can be seen that 1k is 1024 divided by 5 – 204.8 standard typing words.

A single unit is called a byte so a kbyte is 1024 bytes.

Some electronic typewriters have memories just like microcomputers. The only difference is that many memories are much smaller than those in micros although some machines, up to 32K or 204.8 times 32 – 6553.6 standard typing words. Depending on the size of type face being used this is roughly equal to 20 pages of text – enough for most office situations but totally inadequate when it comes to producing an averaged novel or text of 250 000 to 300 000 words. This is roughly equal to 1220-1465K.

Microcomputer memories vary a great deal in size but it is not unusual to find 128-350K per disk drive using single and double density disks. Hard disk drives offer up to 20-40 megabytes of storage – a megabyte being 1 000 000 bytes. The word 'kbyte' is itself a corruption of 'kilobyte'. Each 1Mb (Megabyte) of storage is worth roughly 975K.

Exercise 80

Copy the following article making the required corrections. Use a suitable sheet of paper.

HEADS — Spaced caps.

[margin note: Change the paragraph headings to side/marginal headings typed in capitals without underscore.*]*

["/|:] "What do daisywheels, golf balls and thimbles have in common? The question
[uc/on] could come out of mastermind. The answer is that they are all heads used/
[s] typewriter or printers.

Golf balls. These are now considered to be old fashioned in many circles
but they are still in use. A golf ball head looks like a golf ball in as
[(5)/(7)] much as it is from the top/circular and has rows of keys which look rather
like the 'dimples' on a golf ball. Golf ball heads produce a high quality
[many] copy but the speed of operation is too slow for use with/word processors.

[at/and] Daisywheels. Made of plastic or metal the wheels have spokes at/the end of
[ge] which is a character. The wheels are easily fixed to an appropriate typewriter or printer and can be used to print material at high speed – often
[|-|] bidirectional. This means that the machine does not have to waste time
returning to the left hand margin – it can print from left to right and from
right to left.

Thimbles. These heads look like a daisywheel which has 'died' – or is
[a] trying to imitate a golf ball. Instead of being solid the thimble is made of
curved spokes – the spokes being like those of a 'bent' daisywheel.

[circled margin notes:]
a little
each spoke
which last longer but cost more
like a golf ball

SPECIAL CHARACTERS AND COMBINATION CHARACTERS

The range and number of characters available on any typewriter varies according to the kind of machine it is, the model and the make.

12.1 TYPE BAR MACHINES

Type bar machines have a 'fixed' keyboard, and the one supplied at the time of sale is, to all intents and purposes, constant. The keys are fixed to type bars which are themselves fastened into the machine. The only way of changing the type bars is by removing the fixing wire and inserting the required character bar – a job for an expert. It follows that you should make sure that your type bar machine is fitted with the characters you require at the time of purchase in addition to ensuring that it is the pitch you want (i.e. has the required size of type). If you want more characters than the machine has available you must make substitutes by using a combination of available characters or by writing the characters with a pen.

12.2 MACHINES USING GOLF BALL, DAISYWHEEL AND THIMBLE HEADS

Often called *single element* machines because the printing unit is all in one solid piece, these machines have interchangeable heads and a range of pitches – usually 10, 12 and 15. Most manufacturers offer a wide range of type styles, including proportional spacing, and you are able to select the style and characters as each situation demands – accents, scientific symbols etc. Some machines, unlike type bar machines, offer alternative line spacing to the usual 6 lines per 25 mm (1 in) – 8 lines per 25 mm being the current maximum. Again, if you want more characters than are available on the heads you must make them using combination of available characters or write them.

152

12.3 WORD PROCESSORS

A word processor only handles text, it does not print it. The *hard copy* or text has to be produced on a *printer*. There are a wide variety of printers available. Golf ball, daisywheel and thimble printers offer high quality, though at fairly slow printing speeds – up to 30 characters per second (cps). For high speed printing you need a *dot matrix* printer or an *ink jet* printer. The printing speeds of these are very high (over 200 cps) but the quality is not as good as in single element printers. Combinations of characters can be produced provided the word processor and printer are compatible. In the word processing manual you will find them listed under such headings as *subscript*, *superscript*, *toggle*, *strikeout* and *strikeover*. Special printing effects are also available, such as *bold printing* and *double-strike*.

12.4 COMBINATION CHARACTERS – AND HOW TO MAKE THEM

The following list includes the most commonly used combination characters and you should copy the characters which your machine does not have so that you will know how to produce them.

```
SIGN    NAME OF SIGN AND HOW TO MAKE IT

* (*)   Asterisk.  Turn the roller anticlockwise one 'click'
        or half line space and type a small 'x'.  Back-space
        and type a hyphen over it.  Remember to return to
        the original line of text.

/       Caret.  Type the solidus, back-space and type an
        underscore.

¢       Cedi - an East African unit of currency.  Type a
        capital 'C', back-space and type a solidus over it.

°(°C)   Degrees sign.  Used when typing units of temperature
        or latitude and longitude.  Click back half a line
        (turn the roller anticlockwise) and type a small
        'o'.

÷       Division sign.  Type a hyphen.  Back-space and type
        a colon over it.
```

$\not{S}$ ($)   Dollar sign. Type a capital 'S', back-space and type the solidus through it.

‡   Double dagger - used to indicate footnotes. Turn the roller anticlockwise a half line space and type a capital 'I'. Back-space and use the ratchet release to turn the roller a millimetre before typing another capital 'I' over the first.

=   Equals sign. Type a hyphen and use the ratchet release to turn the roller a millimetre before typing a second hyphen under it - use the back-space.

!   Exclamation mark. Type an apostrophe, back-space and type a full stop under it.

H_2 Inferior character (also called a subscript because it appears below the typing line). Turn the roller anticlockwise half a line space to type the required character.

ℓ Litres sign. Produce it by handwriting unless you have a special key.

$)\overline{}$ Long division. Type a bracket and turn the roller anticlockwise a full line space to type the underscore.

-      Minus sign. Use a hyphen.

x   Multiplication sign. Use a small 'x'.

$^o/_o$ Percentage sign (%). Turn the roller anticlockwise half a line space and type a small 'o'. Return to the typing line and type a solidus and another 'o'.

+   Plus sign. Not always possible to produce. A hyphen with an apostrophe typed through it sometimes works but if not write it in.

£ (₤)   Pounds sign. Not always available on American single element heads. Type a capital 'L', back-space and type an equals sign over it.

§   Section sign. Made like the double dagger but using the capital 'S'.

†   Single dagger - used to indicate footnotes. Turn the roller anticlockwise a half line space. Type a capital 'I', back-space and type a hyphen through it.

]   Square bracket facing left. Type the underscore and then the solidus. Back-space and turn the roller anticlockwise a full line space before typing a second underscore.

[Square bracket facing right. Type the solidus, back-space and type an underscore. Turn the roller anti-clockwise a full line space and type a second underscore.

m³   Superior character (also called a superscript because it appears above the typing line). Turn the roller half a line space to type the required character.

Exercise 81

Set out the test below on a suitable sheet of paper ready for completion by the candidates. Use any consistent style of presentation.

ARITHMETIC TEST

<u>Answer all questions on the paper</u>

<u>Time allowed 15 min</u>

1. £
    295·40 −
    132·27
    ═══

2. $
    2227·79 −
    946·37
    ═══

3. m
    227·26 −
    136·94
    ═══

4. km
    4462·22 −
    1997·33
    ═══

5. cm
    96·70
    12 ×
    ═══

6. $
    346·2 ×
    11
    ═══

7. £
    986·2 ×
    9
    ═══

8. mm
    97 ×
    13
    ══

9. cm
    926 ×
    9
    ══

10. 227 ÷ 18 + 47 − 26 =

11. 92·46 + 27·32 − 18·77 ÷ 10·00 =

12. £228 ÷ 4 × 10 − £28·50 =

13. $338 + $287 ÷ 10 × 12 =

14. 936·50 km + 221·70 km − 136·58 km =

15. 250 cm + 929 cm − 136 cm − 275 cm =

12.5 ACCENTS

Single element machines often have special heads for use when typing
foreign languages which require accents. Some manual and electric/
electronic typewriters are fitted with 'dead' keys which can be used to
type the required accent without moving the typing point – so that the
required letter can be typed over or under the accent as required. If you
are using a word processor, consult the manual. Foreign language keys can
be fitted to type bar machines. They take the place of little-used keys
such as fractions. The only accents which can be produced satisfactorily
on a machine without accents are the *cedilla* and the *umlaut*.

The *cedilla* is produced by typing a comma under 'c' (ç).

The *umlaut* is produced by typing the double quotes (″) over the 'u' –
(ü).

All other accents should be handwritten using an ink or ball-point pen
and matching ink. Examples: acute (´), grave (`), circumflex (^), diaresis
(umlaut) (··), tilde (ñ).

Exercise 82
Type the German passage below on a suitable sheet of paper.

Von frühen Zeiten an war "Deutschland" nur ein
geographischer Ausdruck wie zum Beispiel in
England Wessex, das seit lange her keine
eigentliche Grafschaft gewesen ist. Wie war
denn das? Manche verschiedene deutsche Stämme
haben in geschichtlicher Zeit den geographischen
Raum, der endlich "Deutschland" genannt wurde,
besiedelt, aber dieses grosse Gebiet, das
Brandenburg, Preussen, Bayern, Hessen Sachsen und
viele andere Staaten in sich fasste, war bis 1870
keine politische Einheit.

Bestimmende Faktoren der Einheit der deutschen
Stämme waren sogar im frühesten Zeitalter ohne
Zweifel die deutschen Flüsse - die Oder, die
Elbe, die Weser, die Donau, Der Main und vor
allem der Rhein. Die Flusse waren die
Wasserbahnen der Natur, die den Handel und den
Anschluss zwischen den deutschen Stämmen
mächtig förderten.

158

Exercise 83

Type the French passage on a suitable sheet of paper. Insert the accents with a pen unless your machine has them.

Cette histoire a été écrite par un des écrivains les plus
médiocres de notre ère moderne. Elle vaut quand même être
traduite à l'écriture à cause de l'hétérogénéite mensongère
de ses personnages. L'héroïne s'intitulait de temps à autre
Hélène, mais plus souvent Héloïse. Elle venait d'être reçue
chez les Avézédo, ses amis préférés. Elle s'était vite
installée dans une pièce qu'on lui avait réservée speciale-
ment. C'est juste à l'instant où elle allait sortir de la
pièce que le téléphone a sonné. Elle s'est étonnée de
distinguer la voix de sa grand'mère qu'elle espérait ne plus
revoir qu'après l'événement le plus désespéré de sa vie, son
élévation à la noblesse par le mariage à l'Evêque octo-
génaire d'Evian. Grand'maman s'est écriée: "Je sais tout.
Dès maintenant il faut m'obéir, sinon je vais tout dire."
Héloïse commençait à être inquiète. Elle a répondu d'une
voix aiguë: "Vous m'avez déjouée. C'est que vous êtes très
désobligeante." Elle a appelé le maître d'hôtel et elle a
commandé, sans éveiller en lui le moindre soupçon, un jus de
ciguë. Il l'a apporté à la hâte et elle l'a avalé avide-
ment. La mourante s'est étendue sur le canapé et elle a
expiré. L'évêque a été désolé par cet événement malcontreux
et n'était pas à même de survivre longtemps à cette débâcle
déchirante.

Exercise 84

Type the exercise on a suitable sheet of paper.

THE ACTION OF WATER ON QUICKLIME

If water is added to quicklime some of the water
boils and comes off as steam. The reaction is:

calcium oxide + water = calcium oxide.

$CaO + H_2O = Ca(OH)_2$

and

$O^{2-} + H_2O = 2OH^-$

Exercise 85

Type the following on a suitable sheet of paper in double line spacing.

<u>Work out the following</u>

1. $3[2(x-1)] = 6$
2. $2[4(y+2)] = 9$
3. $3[5(x-7)] = 6$
4. $3 = [6(y-2)(y+3)] - 6$
5. $0 = [5(x-2)(y-1)] + 5$
6. $[(x+y)^3]^2$
7. $3a + 7p = 2(a-p)$
8. $[3(x-6)]^2 = 8$
9. $4[3(x-6)] = 8$
10. $[(p+q)^2]^2$

Exercise 86

Type the following on a suitable sheet of paper.

<u>GLASS</u>

Glass is made from sand, or silica. Sand is heated with sodium carbonate and calcium carbonate (and scrap glass which assists melting). Carbon dioxide is given off and sodium silicate and calcium silicate are formed. The glass also contains some unchanged silica.

$$SiO_2 + Na_2CO_3 = Na_2SiO_3 + CO_2$$

$$SiO_2 + CaCO_3 = CaSiO_3 + CO_2$$

$$SiO_2 + CO_3^{2-} = SiO_3^{2-} + CO_2$$

THE COMPLETION OF
FORMS

Essentially, form completion consists of placing material above a dotted or ruled line, or aligning material with that already printed, or placing material consistently after printed headings. Some electronic typewriters and word processors can do this automatically - see your manual.

13.1 POSITIONING MATERIAL ABOVE A DOTTED OR RULED LINE

Material typed above a dotted or ruled line should be positioned so that the lower case letters which extend below the line of type (g, j, p, q and y) are just clear of the line and are not more than 1.5 mm above it. To do this:

1. Set the machine on 'stencil' so that anything typed does not have to be erased.
2. Press up (if using a type bar manual machine) or type on a low impact setting (if using a single element machine) a lower case g or j.
3. Check to see if the character is positioned correctly. If not, use the *platen release* (sometimes called the *interliner*) to turn the platen (roller) slightly. Press up or type another g or j - and so on until the position is correct.
4. Remove any 'evidence' of your trial run and with the machine back on ribbon (and the impact setting adjusted if necessary) type the required information. The correct position is shown below.

quiet grey pony   quiet grey pony

13.2 POSITIONING MATERIAL AFTER A PRINTED HEADING

Either align on the longest line of the heading/printed material (example on page 163) or align after each heading (example on page 164). To do this:

move the typing point to the last character in the printed heading and tap once for the character and once or twice (depending on the spaces you want to leave after the heading) on the space bar before typing the information. You must be consistent in the number of spaces you leave on any particular document – 1 or 2 being the norm.

13.3 ALIGNMENT WITH PRINTED HEADINGS

This adjustment is the same as for the positioning of material above a dotted or ruled line (see above).

13.4 THE PRODUCTION OF FORMS

Forms to be completed on the typewriter should be produced in double line spacing. Care must be taken to ensure that sufficient space is left for the information to be inserted (messages, addresses, accident particulars, etc.) depending on the nature of the form.

Headings may be produced and space left after them for the later insertion of the desired information.

Lines above which information is to be inserted may be produced using continuous full stops or the underscore. A space should be left after a heading and before the first full stop/underscore as for continuous leader dots.

Deletions on forms
Deletions on forms should be made with the typewriter – not by hand. Use the hyphen, the raised underscore or an upper or lower case 'x'. Only one method should be used on any particular form. If you are using a word processor see *overstrike*. Example page 165.

Exercise 87

Use a sheet of A6 paper (148 × 105 mm) and produce the form below leaving margins of at least 13 mm ($\frac{1}{2}$ in) on each side.

```
PRIZE DAY


Name (Mr/Miss/Mrs/Ms*) _____


I will/will not* be attending on Prize Day.

I will/will not* be bringing (space for number) visitors.

I/we will/will not* require refreshments.

Address     _____


            _____


            _____



* Delete as necessary
```

Complete the form for yourself and imagine that you will be attending with 2 visitors. You will all require refreshments.

13.5 MEMORANDUMS

Memorandums are used in business to convey a range of written or typed information. They are, in effect, notes sent on printed forms. They indicate who the information is from, a reference (if required), to whom the information is addressed, the date and, sometimes, a subject heading. Memorandums do not have, normally, a salutation or a complimentary close.

Exercise 88

Copy the memorandum form shown in Exercise 89 (or design your own using the 'pattern' given) and complete it with the following information. Use suitable margins. *Note*: the information has been blocked on the longest line in each heading.

MEMORANDUM

For use within the Company only

From: Managing Director   Ref: JCM/AFS

To: All Staff   Date: Today's date

FACTORY VISIT BY OVERSEAS CLIENTS

Our Middle Eastern clients who ordered the last SP/YBM/C consignment (and were, incidentally, very pleased with the quality and promptness of delivery) have expressed an interest in placing further orders with us. They are further interested in establishing an assembly plant in their country and would like to visit our factory to see all aspects of production and design. It is proposed that we manufacture parts for assembly by them to save problems with the transportation of finished goods.

I would advise staff that the proposed visit will take place on (28 days from now) and a party of not less than 16 guests can be expected. The party will stay for 2 days and members will be attached to all our main departments for a whole day. The rest of the visit will be as a party.

I know that all staff would wish to ensure the success of this venture which will safeguard jobs for many years to come.

Exercise 89

Copy the memorandum form below or use your own form. Take 2 copies. Mark one copy 'File' and the other 'Chairman'. Note that each 'insertion' has been typed an equal number of spaces from the printed information. Follow this style or that used on the previous page.

MEMORANDUM

From Managing Director .... Ref DSM/LS ....

To Departmental Heads .... Date 6 June (this year) ....

Subject Reference Sources ....

A Chamber of Commerce discussion about the use of reference sources in businesses such as our prompts me to raise the matter at our next monthly meeting. I would like to have a close look at our provision.

As a company we spend a lot of money on Research and Development but we have no central spending plan on reference sources and we seem to rely upon individual Departmental Heads to take the initiative in their own area. With the advent of the new micro technology I think we should give serious thought to the establishment of a central reference section, properly fund and staff it and link in to whatever electronic information banks come along.

Can Departmental Heads send me a note of their current provision and what, if any, expansion they would like to see?

Exercise 90
Produce 2 copies of the form below and complete one with the information which has been typed on it. Complete the second form for Mr Peter William Cooper who lives at 45 Boundary Way, Your town. His telephone number is 99881 and he is 17 years old. He wants Course 34A, Oil Painting.

REGISTRATION FORM

First name(s)   Joyce

Surname   Stephens

Address   Flat 23

Connaught House

Boundary Way

Your town

Telephone number   6349

Age (if under 18)

Status (M̶r̶/Mrs/M̶i̶s̶s̶/M̶s̶)

Course(s) required   397 - Photography

Exercise 91
Complete a memorandum form using the following copy. From: Chief Accountant; To: Sales Director; Date: 23 May (this year); Ref: JAC/PAW; Subject: Credit. Take a carbon copy and mark it 'Managing Director'.

I am concerned to find just how much it has cost the Company to give extended credit to our customers. At times during the current financial year the interest on capital lost by giving extended credit was more than our gross profit margins. (Paragaraph) I have spoken to the Managing Director and he has agreed that until the matter can be raised at a full board meeting we will not offer more than four weeks' credit. I know this will cause a few problems but it is essential that we tighten up.

Exercise 92

Copy the accident form on a suitable sheet of paper.

ACCIDENT FORM

First name(s) _____

Surname _____

Policy number _____

Place of accident and time _____

_____

Weather conditions - state condition of the road _____

_____

Name and address of the owner of the vehicle involved _____

_____

_____

Name and address of the driver of the other vehicle involved
if different from the above:

_____

_____

Were the Police called? If 'yes' state name(s) and number(s)
of the officers involved.

_____

Give full particulars of the accident and provide a sketch of
the accident scene. Use a separate sheet if necessary.

Complete the above form making up the necessary detail. (Add any items
you think the form should include such as estimates of the amount of
damage involved, where your vehicle currently is, etc.)

13.6 **POSTCARDS**

Postcards may be used for sending a range of non-confidential information, often of a standard nature, which means that some information can be pre-printed on the cards for later completion by the typist. Postcards should conform to the current postal regulations so far as size and weight are concerned. The exercises in this book are based on the A6 size (148 x 105 mm).

To produce a postcard on the typewriter:

Set margins of at least 13 mm (pica 5-53; elite 6-64; 15 pitch 8-80). Turn up to leave 13 mm ($\frac{1}{2}$ in) blank at the top of the card and type the name and address of the firm or organisation sending it across the full width. Use single line spacing. Include the telephone number and type it in any suitable position.

Turn up 2 single lines and type the reference (if any) at the left margin and back-space the date to type it flush on the right margin. If there is no reference, the date can be typed at the left margin. Turn up 3 single lines and type the required information in the blocked or the indented style.

Address postcards as you would envelopes - see pages 28-30.

168

Exercise 93
Type the postcard below on A6 card following the directions given on the previous page. Send it to Miss Susan Walker, 23 High Street, Your town.

```
Sports & Social Club, Memorial Ground, Park Lane, Your
town.                                    Telephone 22387

23 July (this year)

Dear Susan

You have been selected to play for the 1st team away
against Northern on Saturday (date next Saturday).
The team will meet at the Club House at 1.00 pm.

If you are unable to play please telephone me at home
(83345) as soon as possible.

Yours sincerely
Match Secretary
```

The card may be signed - if so leave space for the signature and type in the name of the sender.

Exercise 94

Type this postcard on a sheet of A6 card.

```
The Camera Centre, Camera House, Madeira Road, Your town.
Telephone 29381


Reference                           Date as postmark


Dear Sir/Madam


We would advise that your (leave space for the make)
camera serial number (leave space for the number) has now
been examined by our repair department.

We estimate that the repair will take (leave space for
the number) days to complete and will cost (leave space
for the amount).  We await your further instructions.


Yours faithfully
(leave a blank line for the signature)
D Singh
Repairs Department Manager
```

Complete the above card with the following details. Reference: 23/901.
Make of camera: Olympus OM-2N. Serial number: 7-8934C/MN3. The
repair will take 7 days to repair and will cost 56.50 (£s or $s depending
on your choice!). Send it to Mrs A Wright, 34 Parklands Avenue, Your
town.

Exercise 95

Type this postcard on a sheet of A6 card.

```
From: Central College of Higher Education, Victoria Road, Your
town.  Tele: 892534
Date: 10 September (this year)   Ref: AO/85/983


Dear (leave space for the name)
I thank you for your recent application to join the (leave
space for the name of the course) course which commences on
(leave space for the date).  You are invited to attend for an
interview at the above address on (leave space for the date).
You should initially report to reception.  (Paragraph)  Will
you please telephone your intention as to whether you will
attend the interview or not?   Yours faithfully   Registrar
```

Send the above postcard to Mr Peter Andrews, 45 Croft Street, Your town. He is invited to attend for interview on 17 September following his application to join the Communications course on 5 September. The course commences on 2 October this year.

13.7 DOCUMENTS USED IN BUSINESS TRANSACTIONS

While individuals conduct most business transactions with little more paperwork than a receipt from a till showing their purchases at a particular time, businesses must keep written records. Increasingly these are produced on computers or word processors with appropriate programs – but many are still handwritten or typed.

Orders

Orders are usually made on pre-printed forms which may show:

The name and address of the firm or company ordering the goods.
The name and address of the supplier.
The date.
The order number – for the orderer's records.
The reference or catalogue number of the goods required.
A description of the goods – size, colour, etc.
The price – although this is often omitted.
Any special conditions of the order – delivery dates, etc.

The typist fills in the details as appropriate, taking care to ensure that the catalogue numbers in particular are correct. Usually one or more copies of orders are taken; one for the supplier, one for the records office of the ordering firm and one for the department requiring the goods.

Advice and delivery notes

Advice notes are sometimes sent to the firm ordering the goods to say when goods can be expected. The note may state when the goods will be despatched, the means of delivery (own vehicles or rail, etc.), what goods will be sent, the number of packages, etc. An advice note is a form of acknowledgement of an order.

Delivery notes are enclosed with goods delivered. A delivery note will show what has been delivered (quantity, description, etc.) and will contain space for signature by the representative of the firm accepting delivery. This person should check each delivery against the delivery note before signing but if this is not practicable they should sign the note to the effect that the goods have been delivered but not checked. Any damaged or missing items should be recorded – or notified later.

Invoices

Invoices actually charge for goods delivered. An invoice will list the order number, the delivery and invoice date, the number of items delivered, a description of the goods, their unit price, the total price for each item, the total for the invoice, any discounts allowed, any taxes due, the terms of payment and the sum due for that particular invoice. As the typist/ word processor operator produces the invoice he or she often produces the advice note and the delivery note at the same time plus copies of the invoice for their own firm's records. The information on an invoice may be exactly the same as that on an advice note and delivery note with the exception that any reference to price will be blanked out - often by omitting the carbon from the relevant columns. These documents are often produced in packs and the typist must take care to avoid errors - see page 42 for instructions on how to correct packs of documents.

Any errors in an invoice must be corrected using debit and credit notes.

A debit note is sent when an insufficient amount has been charged for goods - it is in effect a demand for an extra payment. Firms often ensure that they can do this by printing or typing the letters E & OE at the foot of invoices, which means 'Errors and Omissions Excepted'.

A credit note is a kind of refund for damaged or returned goods - and for crates or other containers.

Details of debit and credit notes are recorded on statements.

Statements

From time to time, usually monthly, firms send statements to customers. A statement shows the position which exists between a supplier and a customer at a given time. The first item usually shows the balance from the previous statement and then lists, in date order, goods sent, goods returned and goods paid for. The final sum is the amount due at the time the statement was despatched. It follows that any payment which is, for example, in the post will not be recorded. Both firms should check statements to confirm what has happened.

The documents shown below are fairly typical of an order, an invoice and a statement. You should reproduce them on suitable sheets of paper in order to carry out the exercises which follow - or use other relevant forms.

The completion of business documents is the same as for the completion of forms - see page 160. It is usual to produce money columns in these documents as described on page 114, though the final total on a statement is not totalled.

Example 37

ORDER NUMBER

Customer	Supplier

Date

Please supply the following goods

Number Required	Description of goods	Reference Number	List Price

Delivery address if different from customer's ....

Example 38

WHOLESALE SUPPLIES LTD
UNIT 3
INDUSTRIAL ESTATE

INVOICE NO _____

DATE _____

ORDER NO _____

TERMS _____

Supplied to:

Number	Description	Unit Price	Total Price

E & OE

174

Example 39

WHOLESALE SUPPLIES LTD
UNIT 3
INDUSTRIAL ESTATE

STATEMENT OF ACCOUNT

Date _____

Customer _____

Date	Ref No	Item	Debit	Credit	Balance

The last amount in the balance column is the amount due

Exercise 96

Use a copy of the order form shown in Example 37 or another suitable order form and complete it with the following information.

Order Number 871   Date: 18 June (this year)

Customer: Fowler & Sons   Supplier: Wholesale Supplies Ltd
          23 High Street   Unit 3
          (Your town)   Industrial Estate
                              (Your town)

Number Required	Description of Goods	Reference Number	List Price
1	32K electronic memory typewriter	RS882/32	1120.00
2 boxes	Correctable ribbons for the above	CR882	25.00
1 box	Lift-off ribbons for the above	LR/882	21.00

Exercise 97

Use a copy of the invoice shown in Example 38 or another suitable invoice and complete with the following information which is related to the above order.

Invoice Number 9923   Date 27 June (this year)

Supplied to: Fowler & Sons   Terms $2\frac{1}{2}$% monthly account
            23 High Street
            (Your town)   Order Number 871

Number	Description	Unit Price	Total Price
1	RS882/32 typewriter	1120.00	1120.00
2 boxes	CR882 correctables	25.00	50.00
1 box	LR/882 lift-offs	21.00	21.00
			1191.00
	Less 10% trade discount		119.10
			1071.90
	Add VAT @ 15%		160.78
			1232.68

Exercise 98

Use a copy of the order form shown in Example 37 or your own form and complete it with the following.

Order Number: 331C. Customer: Carlsons Electrics, The Arcade, Terminal Shopping Centre, Your town. Supplier: Wholesale Supplies Ltd, Unit 3, Industrial Estate, Your town. Date: 3 April (this year).

Number Required	Description of Goods	Reference Number	List Price
10	Radio/Recorder	TS34/221D	120.00
20	Video Recorder	TSVR993D	250.00
2	Hi-Fi deck	TS/424/HD	150.00
1	Hi-Fi deck	YN0882	175.00

Exercise 99

Use a copy of the invoice shown in Example 38 or your own form and complete it with the following information which is related to the above order.

Invoice Number: 7889. Order Number: 331C. Date: 28 April (this year). Supplied to: Carlsons Electrics, The Arcade, Terminal Shopping Centre, Your town. Terms: Monthly account net.

Number	Description	Unit Price	Total Price
10	TS34/221D	120.00	1200.00
20	TSVR993D	250.00	5000.00
2	TS/424/HD	150.00	300.00
1	YN0882	175.00	175.00
			6675.00
		Less 25% Trade discount	1668.00
			5007.00
		Plus VAT @ 15%	751.05
		Total	5758.05

Exercise 100

Use a copy of the Statement of Account shown in Example 39 or one of your own and complete it with the following information. This Statement relates to the Invoice on page 175.

Statement of Account Number: 23. Date: 1 July (this year).
Customer: Fowler & Sons, 23 High Street, Your town.

Date	Ref No	Item	Debit	Credit	Balance
31 May		Balance b/d			967.45
4 June		Cheque		595.32	372.13
8 June	8750	Goods	895.87		1268.00
14 June	190	Returns		175.56	1092.44
16 June	8825	Goods	790.00		1882.44
21 June		Cheque		967.47	914.97
22 June	222	Returns		5.50	909.47
27 June	9923	Goods	1232.68		2142.15
28 June		Cheque		750.75	1391.40

Exercise 101

Use a copy of the Statement of Account shown in Example 39 or one of your own and complete it with the following information.

Statement Number: 83. Date: 2 May (this year).
Customer: Carlsons Electrics, The Arcade, Terminal Shopping Centre, Your town.

Date	Ref No	Item	Debit	Credit	Balance
31 March		Balance b/d			2964.50
4 April	6250	Goods	951.25		3915.75
7 April	407	Returns		362.80	3552.95
9 April		Cheque		2964.50	588.45
11 April	6671	Goods	1850.95		2439.40
17 April	472	Returns		135.00	2304.40
18 April	307	Debit Note	290.00		2594.40
28 April	7899	Goods	5758.05		8352.45
29 April	804	Returns		175.00	8177.45

CHAPTER 14

ABBREVIATIONS

There are two kinds of abbreviations in common use: *standard abbreviations*, which may be produced in their abbreviated form, and *manuscript abbreviations*, which should be typed in full. The 'boundary' between the two kinds is somewhat arbitrary.

14.1 MANUSCRIPT ABBREVIATIONS

These are short forms used by individuals when taking down or writing notes for later expansion. The range varies from individual to individual and the list below is by no means exhaustive. Manuscript abbreviations should always be typed in full. Many individuals simply remove the vowels (a, e, i, o and u) from words.

Word	Abbreviation	Word	Abbreviation
account	a/c	pages	pp
amount	amt	received	recd
and	&	receipt	recpt
been	bn	reference	ref
because	bec	secretary	sec
building	bldg	shall	sh
credit	cr	should	shd
debit/dear	dr	the	t or /
department	dept	that	th
expenses	exs	together	togthr
faithfully	ffly	very	v
for	f	will	wl
from	fr	with	w
have	hv	which	wh
-ing	g	would	wd
paid	pd	you	y
page	p	your, year	yr

Take a copy of the above list on a suitable sheet of paper. It will be seen that these abbreviations are only a sample of an endless range, but the above list covers those used in most public examinations. See page 27 for the use of the ampersand (&).

When producing accounts the abbreviations a/c, dr and cr may be left in their abbreviated form. Dr for Debit should not be confused with Dr when used for Doctor or Dear. Honorary Secretary is often abbreviated to Hon Sec and should always be typed in full.

14.2 STANDARD ABBREVIATIONS

Standard abbreviations are those which are universally acceptable in their shortened form. Any good dictionary will have lists of them and individuals should always use a dictionary when in doubt. The list of standard abbreviations, like all other aspects of language, is constantly growing. The following is a tiny fraction of the many hundreds of standard abbreviations and each area of study has its own particular list, chemical equations, mathematical symbols, etc.

A	ACF	b	bhp	Bt	CJ	DA
AA	ACGB	BA	BL	BVB	CO	DCL
AAA	ACI	Bart	BLitt	C	c/o	DP
AAF	ACIS	BB	BM	CA	cod	DPh
AAG	AD	BBC	BMus	CAB	COI	DSc
AAI	Ad fin	BC	BP	cap	Col	E
AB	Adjt	BCom	Bp	caps	coll	E & OE
Abp	Adm	BD	Bros	Capt	Co-op	EEC
AC	AFA	BDS	BSc	Card	Corp	EFTA
ACA	AFAS	BEd	BSI	CC	cp	Esq

The above list gives a small idea of the vast number of standard abbreviations and no one can be expected to know them all. Keep your own list – and remember that each aspect of life has its own particular standard abbreviations.

14.3 POST OFFICE ABBREVIATIONS

In addition to manuscript and standard abbreviations the Post Office has its own lists (see also page 31). A browse through any telephone directory will reveal abbreviations particular to telecommunications. The list below is a small sample of the Post Office abbreviations in common usage.

Colorado (Colo)	Avenue (Av)	Cottage (Cot)
East (E)	Bank (Bnk)	Chambers (Chambs)
Gibralta (Gib)	Close (Clo)	Drive (Dv)
Iowa (Ia)	Court (Ct)	Estate (Est)
Illinois (Ill)	Crescent (Cres)	Farm (Fm)

14.4 COMPANIES AND PARTNERSHIPS

The letters Ltd (Limited) denote a limited company – a private limited company in the UK as opposed to plc (PLC) denoting a public limited company. In the USA the letters Inc (Incorporated) take the place of the UK plc, while in Australia Pty Ltd (Property Limited) is used. Messrs (Messieurs) indicates a partnership (and should never be used with Ltd or plc). Co is the abbreviated form of Company.

14.5 MANUSCRIPT

In many public examinations questions are handwritten for candidates to 'decipher'. As a rule only simple manuscript abbreviations are included and except for the higher levels of examinations candidates are not expected to distinguish between standard and manuscript abbreviations. If you are preparing for public examinations you should practise typing from a range of handwriting styles.

Exercise 102
Type the exercise below on a suitable sheet of paper and expand the
manuscript abbreviations.

BEES

Town dwellers probably know v little abt bees
& care even less, except wh they go on
holiday & are 'pestered' by a rather large, buzzing
fly wh can sting. Country dwellers & farmers
(particularly fruit farmers) know tht bees are
v important. Without them essential crops are not
pollinated & yields drop dramatically. So
important are they tht farmers wl often import
hives of bees to pollinate crops at t appropriate
time of t yr. [There are many kinds of bees
ranging fr t killer bees of Central America to t
humble 'bumble bee' wh lives on its own & is a
familiar sight in English summers. Commercially
bees are kept in hives wh come in all shapes
& sizes & make t collection of honey bth
more reliable & safer. T flavour of t honey
depends on t flowers t bees collect their
pollen fr. [Most children learn tht a swarm of
bees in May is worth a load of hay; a swarm of
bees in June is worth a silver spoon but tht a
swarm of bees in July isn't worth a fly.

Exercise 103

Copy the following article and expand the abbreviations as required. Use a suitable sheet of paper.

FACETS OF MAN

In early 1983 an American satellite became t first man made object to leave our planetary system. On the satellite is a diagram of our solar system + t outline of a naked man + woman. T idea is th if there are other life forms in t universe they may one day find t object + learn a little (v little!) about t dominant life form on t planet we know as t earth. [W t man-in-t-st probably does not realise is how little is known abt t ordinary men + women wh lived in man's recent past. Many people are curious abt t origin of man t species + gaze at pictures in bks + magazines or at models in museums - but reality is probably far removed from wh appears to be evidence. [Early evidence of man's physical characteristics comes fr fossils but these are few + far between, they are v fragmentary + may nt be wholly representative of t population. Later t Egyptians perfected t art of preserving bodies + so w know fly accurately how they looked. [For t most part w hv to rely on wks of art, painting + sculpture, to give us some idea of how people looked + dressed - coins also give a few clues. Written records provide some further evidence. Wh we do nt know is how these people sounded whn they spoke + wh they really looked like - sculpture, pictures + writings can all too easily flatter. [Future man wl knw a lt more abt us frm films + recordings.

Exercise 104

Take a copy of the following article and note the content for future use. Expand the manuscript abbreviations as required. Use a suitable sheet of paper.

BACKFEEDING

Sometimes called backward feed

A typist may be called upon to make one or more corrections on a sheet of paper wh has bn fastened, at t top, in a sheaf of papers.

To do this:

(i) Put a sheet of paper into the machine as usual.

(ii) Place t _bottom_ of t sheet t be corrected betwn t sheet of paper alrdy in t machine & t roller or platen.

(iii) Turn t roller as though to wind t original sheet out of t machine. As y do so t sheet t be corrected wl be wound into t machine.

Use the paper release lever t align t sheet t be corrected, remove t error & mke t correction. The correction may involve t use of squeezing or spreading techniques.

CUTTING & PASTING

Sometimes a tpst may hv t mke substantial corrections t documents & t only practical soln is t type t correctn on a sheet o matchg paper, cut it out & paste it over t error. T whole sheet cn thn be photocopied & a stncl mstr mde f duplicatg purposes. One advntge of wd prcssrs is th correctns of this nature can be mde on t scrn w v little effort.

FOOTNOTES

Footnotes enable those producing a range of material (reports and texts for examples) either to indicate their sources of information or to add to that given in the text. The reader then has the option of reading or ignoring the footnotes. There are 2 kinds of footnotes: those produced in general typed material and those produced with material which is to be printed.

15.1 FOOTNOTES IN TYPED MATERIAL

A symbol (asterisk, single dagger, double dagger, etc.) or a number is typed, *without a space* between it and the material which precedes it, at the precise point at which a reference is to be made. The symbol or number is typed half a line space above the line of type (see pages 186 and 187), though a machine-produced asterisk will be typed automatically in the correct position. (If you are using a word processor look in your manual under *superscript*.) At the foot of the page the symbol or number is reproduced and a space is left after it before the information is typed in single line spacing, with a blank line between different footnotes. Within a footnote the material may be blocked on the first letter or the second and subsequent lines may be typed from the margin.

Care must be taken to ensure that sufficient space is left at the foot of a page for the footnotes to be inserted. A line of continuous underscores is typed from margin to margin or edge to edge of the page (use the margin release key) between the text and the footnotes. Leave at least one blank line after the underscored line, i.e. turn up at least one single line before the underscored line and 2 single lines after it.

15.2 FOOTNOTES FOR A PRINTER

The footnote symbol is typed in the text as described above but at the end of the line on which the symbol or number appears return the carriage and type an underscored line from edge to edge of the page or from margin to margin. Turn up 2 single lines and type the footnote – as described above. After typing the footnote return the carriage and repeat the underscored line. Turn up 2 single lines and continue with the text.

Examples of both methods will be found in the following exercises.

Exercise 105

Copy this exercise with footnotes on to a suitable sheet of paper. Use double line spacing for the text and single for the footnotes. These are footnotes for typed material.

```
M O D E R N   T Y P E W R I T E R S
```

Some of the latest electronic typewriters require different skills than the 'old fashioned' manual machines which were the latest 'state of the art' only a few years ago. One advantage of these manual machines over some electronic machines is their capacity to work at almost any temperature. Some electronic typewriters require specific temperature and humidity ranges in which to operate* and while no operator likes to work in extremely hot/cold humid temperatures there are times when they must. Should the electricity fail electric/electronic machines are useless and apart from the fact that they will not work some create problems[‡] which the old manual machine operators would never have dreamed of.

While it is true that modern electronic typewriters are much easier, for the mechanics to service, because they have fewer moving parts to wear out[‡] they can prove very expensive. Any reasonably competent individual could repair an old manual machine - now more sophisticated skills are needed.

---

* Xerox 600 range specifies 10^0-32^0 at 15%-85% at altitudes up to 1800 m.

[‡] Many memory machines lose what is in their memory.

[‡] A modern electronic machine has single figure moving parts.

Exercise 106
Copy the footnotes as if for a printer on to a suitable sheet of paper. Use double line spacing for the article and single line spacing for the footnotes.

EDWARD JENNER

One feature of 'the old days' was plague in its various forms and one disease[1] stood out from the rest - smallpox. To

---

[1] Perhaps only leprosy caused such an immediate reaction on the part of others. This disease, which still exists, was not confined to the hotter parts of the world.

---

catch smallpox was almost certain death and the disease swept through whole populations very quickly. Edward Jenner[2]

---

[2] Jenner was a pupil of John Hunter.

---

noticed that farmworkers handling cattle caught cowpox which caused them to develop blisters for a few days. The workers did not appear to suffer any other problems with cowpox and Jenner also noticed that they did not catch smallpox. He theorised that there was a connection between the two and eventually[3] he began to give people cowpox as protection

---

[3] In 1798 he tried to give smallpox to a boy he had already given cowpox to to test his theories.

---

against smallpox. Today the disease has been wiped out.

188

Exercise 107

Type the article with footnotes on a suitable sheet of paper. Type the manuscript abbreviations in full.

PRECIOUS STONES

MASAAI

In modern Nairobi Masaai spears sell alongside a wide range of gems + semi-precious stones, some polished and shaped, others uncut, in jewellery or souvenir shops. Rubies, sapphires, aquamarines, rose[1] garnets and Kenya green garnets[2] have made Nairobi an African gem centre. Apart from t previously mentioned gems + stones, others are smuggled to t Nairobi market. [Accordg to one report[3] t value of gemstone prdctn doubled between 1978 + 1979. Added to tn output must be t prdctn of corundum[4] fr t reopened ruby mine in 1980. Th mine hd bn closed after nationalisation bt it hd returned to its original owner, John Saul. [Ruby mines are found in t far sth of Kenya nr t town of Voi. Tsavorite is generally considered to be a gd substitute f emeralds. T gem belt extends into Tanzania wh Tanzanite is found.

---

(1) Sometimes called rhodolite garnets

(2) Called Tsavorite

(3) Kenya Economic Survey 1980

(4) Rubies, sapphires and emery — an abrasive material used to make emery cloth.

Exercise 108

Type the article as though for a printer on a suitable sheet of paper. Use double line spacing for the article and single line spacing for the footnotes. Type the manuscript abbreviations in full.

MORE FOOD?

The rapid population explosion throughout t world*

* It is a mistake to think th all countries are going thrgh a current ppltn explsn. Some ppltns are static while others are declining.

has led man t consider all sorts of ways & means of increasg fd prdtn. Plants hv bn devrlpd wh yield v. heavy crops & tolerate a wide climatic variation. One stdy currently beg. undertaken is t prdn of crops wh wl tolerate salt water.† These plants are called

† The Food and Agriculture Organisation estimates th there are 3.8 million sq mls of saline soils in t world compared to t 6.0 million sq mls under crop.

halophytes‡ and t group includes some wild species.

‡ From the Greek 'halo' meaning salt & 'phyte' meaning water.

of barley, wheat, sorghum, rice, millet, sugar beet & tomato as well as forage (animal feed) plants such as alfalfa. [One place wh experiments are takg place is Arizona in the United States of America wh salt water fr t Gulf of Mexico is beg used t irrigate crops. A wide rnge of crops are beg grwn - first results suggest th t technique & crops hv got potential. It may well be th future generations wl dine off crops wh we do not at present consider edible - many of wh currently grow naturally in t salt oceans of t globe.

ITINERARIES

There are 2 kinds of itineraries in use: appointments and travel.

16.1 APPOINTMENTS ITINERARIES

Appointments itineraries are usually produced on A6 (148 x 105 mm) paper so that they can be carried in the pocket. They serve to remind the carrier where he or she is supposed to be at a given time – usually during a period of a day. To produce them:

1. Use margins of at least 13 mm ($\frac{1}{2}$ in), as for postcards (see page 167).
2. Turn up 4 single lines to begin and type the name of the person concerned together with any introductory information.
3. Turn up 2 (or 3) single lines and using side/marginal headings (see page 6) for the time of each appointment type the appointments in time order in single line spacing with a blank line between timings.

Example 40
Type this example on a sheet (or card) of A6 paper (148 × 105 mm).

```
ITINERARY

Mr John Fletcher (tomorrow)


0930    Beeny & Co Ltd, Tower House, Ashmore Park,
        Mrs R Jackson, Secretary to Chairman.

1100    Sutton Plastics plc, Unit 2 Trading Estate,
        Mr E Worsey, Research Chemist.

1300    Lunch at Grange Hotel, Porchester Drive, lunch
        with Mr H Baines, Mr R Plumb and Mr T Crowther
        of Aimcarp Ltd.

1530    Messrs Holmes & Rogers, Printing Works, Gordon
        Street, Mr W Walton, Chief Buyer.
```

16.2 TRAVEL ITINERARIES

Travel itineraries cover a longer period of time than do appointments itineraries. They are usually typed on A4 paper using side/marginal headings for the days/timings. Turn up 7 single lines to start. Use suitable margins and single line spacing and leave a blank line between items.

Exercise 109

Copy this travel itinerary on to a sheet of A4 paper following the instructions given on the previous page.

ITINERARY

Mr John Winckler - Sales Week in London 11-15 September

Day	Activity

Monday 11

0957 hrs	Arrive at Euston Hotel and walk to Cora Hotel in Woburn Place. Book in.
1100 hrs	Meeting at Cora Hotel with Mr H Terry, Sales Manager of RKL plc. Continue discussions over lunch at 1300 hrs. Papers in File A.
1800 hrs	Meeting at Park Hotel in Euston Road with Mr S Wright, Sales Manager, Wood & Sons. Papers in File B.

Tuesday 12

0930 hrs	Meeting at LVW Supplies Ltd, Grays Inn Road. Mr C Day, Director. Papers in File C.
1400 hrs	Meeting at Coates Bros Ltd, Grafton Way, with Mrs W Miller, Sales Director. Papers in File D.
1830 hrs	Visit the Trade Exhibition, Strand Hotel, Clarence Gardens.

Wednesday 13

1000 hrs	Meeting at Cora Hotel with Mr P Asburn and Mr T Newton of Tycoate International plc. To be joined over lunch and for the afternoon session by sales staff from Tycoate. Papers in File E.
1800 hrs	Meeting with Mr J Procter, Sales Manager of Pringle & Brown Co Ltd, at Cora Hotel. Papers in File F.

Thursday 14

1030 hrs	Arrive at Imperial Hotel in Copenhagen Street for day visit to the International Trade Fair.

Friday 15

0930 hrs	Meeting at Anglo-African Ltd in Regent Square with Mr A Sabin, Sales Manager. Papers in File G.
1340 hrs	Depart Euston station for home.

Exercise 110

Type this travel itinerary on a sheet of A4 paper.

ITINERARY

Heart of England Tour

Day   Activity.

1. Arrive Birmingham International Airport and then by coach to Stratford-upon-Avon. Book in at Hilton Hotel. Rest of day free for sight seeing.

2. Morning drive to Banbury for coffee and on to Oxford for lunch and afternoon tour of the town. Return to Stratford-upon-Avon via Woodstock and Shipston-on-Stour.

3. Free day in Stratford with optional visits to Shakespeare's birthplace and the Theatre.

4. Drive to Broadway, Cheltenham (for lunch) and return via Stow-on-the-Wold and Morton-in-Marsh.

5. Free day in Stratford with optional river cruise and trip to Anne Hathaway's cottage.

6. Drive to Evesham, Tewkesbury and on to Worcester for evening meal cruising on the river Severn

7. Morning drive to Henley-in-Arden for coffee and on to Warwick for lunch with afternoon free to shop or visit castle.

8. Drive through Birmingham to Sutton Coldfield and thence to Lichfield for lunch with rest of day free. Optional tour of the Cathedral.

9. Free day with optional visit to Coventry and the Cathedral.

10. Morning free. Depart for Birmingham International Airport at 1600 hrs.

194

Exercise 111

Type these appointments itineraries on sheets of A6 (148 × 105 mm) paper or A6 card if it is available.

```
ITINERARY

Miss Elizabeth Marszalek 16 April


0930     Nursing home, 1 Golf Course Road.  Dr (Mrs) V
         Patel, Senior Medical Officer.

1130     Radiology Department, Kwato Road.  Prof A W
         Jukubowski, Senior Hospital Medical Officer.

1300     Lunch with Dr C Das, Senior Lecturer of the
         Department of Obstetrics and Gynaecology in
         the staff canteen.

1530     Maternity Department, Kankiya Street.
         Mrs P Soyebo, Ward Sister.

1645     Telephone office for any messages.
```

ITINERARY
Mr D E Ridley   2 October

0845   Collect mail from sorting office in
        Horden Road and telephone Mr A Mann
        at Head Office.

0930   Temple Office Services, Woodland Avenue.
        Miss P Wickham, Sales Manageress.

1115   Wyvern Interiors Ltd, Cornwall Road.
        Mr T Jenkins. Accountant.

1330   Furniture Trade Sales (1981) Ltd Arden
        Road. Mrs A Anderson and Mr M Woolley
        Directors.

1530   Telephone Regional office for messages.

Exercise 112

Type this travel itinerary on a sheet of A4 paper.

TOUR NO 436
GREECE — 15 DAYS

Day	Activity
1	Arrive at Athens airport and be met by coach to be taken to Hotel Atlantis for lunch. Afternoon free to tour Athens.
2	Morning in Athens. Optional trip to city sights. Afternoon by coach along the Apollo coast to Cape Sounion. Visit Sounion's Temple of Poseidon.
3	Free day in Athens. At 1800 hrs depart by coach to Piraeus for cruise to Heraklion. Dinner on the "Xania" and cruise through the night. Cabins reserved.
4	Arrive at Heraklion and transfer by coach to Ierapetra and Hotel Blue Spell.
5–10	Free.
11	Depart by coach at 1700 hrs for Heraklion and return to Piraeus. Dinner on board. Cabins reserved.
12	Early morning arrival in Piraeus – breakfast on "Xania" first before coach drive to Delphi via Leradia. Book in at Hotel Marathon.
13	Morning drive to Antirion and on to Rion, Patras, Pirgos and Olympia for overnight stay at Hotel Faros.
14	Morning free in Olympia. Afternoon drive to Mycenae and Neuplia. Book in at Hotel Norida.
15	Sightseeing in Corinth and then drive to Athens for return flights in the afternoon.

DOCUMENTS CONNECTED
WITH MEETINGS

People involved in holding meetings find it valuable to keep records and to plan the framework of future meetings. The documents most commonly used are the notice of the meeting, the agenda to be followed at the meeting and the record of the meeting – the minutes. Meetings may be fairly frequent, as in departmental meetings at work, or those of a sports or social club, etc. or they may be of an annual nature.

17.1 NOTICE OF MEETING

It is usual to send members of a committee a notice advising them of the meeting. The notice will give the date, time and place of the meeting.

17.2 AGENDA

At the same time as the notice of the meeting is sent out it is usual to include the agenda, or programme of events, to be followed at the meeting. An agenda provides a framework for the orderly conduct of a meeting and it enables those going to the meeting to plan for it.

It is usual to produce the notice of the meeting and the agenda on the same sheet of paper, though the person responsible for producing copies of either document might be advised to produce spare copies of the agenda in case members forget or lose their copies.

A notice of a meeting and an agenda can be produced on any suitable sheet of paper. The size chosen will depend on the length of the notice and the length of agenda. It is usual to type the name and/or address of the person calling the meeting at the head of the sheet as for a letter and to type the date in a similar fashion. The notice of the meeting and the agenda may be typed, as with letters, in the blocked or the indented style. It is not usual to include a salutation, but to type the notice of the meeting directly after the date. See Exercise 113 for an example.

To type an agenda under a notice of a meeting, turn up 2 single lines after the notice and type the heading 'Agenda' at the left margin (blocked style) or centred over the typing line (semi-blocked style). The items in the agenda are then listed in the order it is proposed to take them at the meeting. Use single line spacing with a blank line between items.

The usual order of an agenda is:

1. Apologies for absence.
2. Minutes of the last meeting – to remind members of what took place.
3. Matters arising from the minutes, such as unfinished business or business upon which action was required.
4. Correspondence.
5. Reports and general business – anything which members have previously indicated that they wish to raise.
6. Any other business – a time when matters not previously notified can be raised.
7. Date, time and place of the next meeting, if known.
8. The name and designation of the person sending out the notice and agenda. The document may be signed. Any enclosures will be indicated in the usual fashion as for a letter.

17.3 CHAIRMAN'S AGENDA

A chairman's agenda is sometimes produced to assist the running of a meeting. In addition to the information given on the agenda produced for the rest of the meeting the chairman's agenda contains other relevant information.

To produce a chairman's agenda:

1. Divide the typing line into 2.
2. Down the left side produce the usual agenda.
3. Opposite each item in the agenda set out the extra information required to assist the chairman.

The exercises on pages 201 and 202 are typical of a chairman's agenda.

Exercise 113

Copy this notice of a meeting and agenda on a suitable sheet of paper. It
is set out in the blocked style.

```
UNION SPORTS AND SOCIAL CLUB                    Telephone 78972
Parklands Avenue
Your town

11 April (this year)

The next General Committee meeting of the Union Sports and
Social Club will be held in the Committee Room at the centre
in Parklands Avenue on 21 April at 1900 hrs.

AGENDA

1  Apologies for absence

2  Minutes of the last meeting held on 19 March (this year)

   Matters arising from the minutes:

   (a)  Sponsorship
   (b)  Grass cutting equipment
   (c)  Surfacing of the tennis courts

4  Secretary's report and correspondence

5  Treasurer's report

6  Team Captains' reports:

   (a)  Hockey
   (b)  Football
   (c)  Tennis
   (d)  Cricket

7  Any other business

8  Date, time and place of the next meeting

Barbara Morris
Minutes Secretary
```

Exercise 114
Copy this notice of a meeting and agenda. Use a suitable sheet of paper. It is set out in the semi-blocked style. You may wish to set it out in the blocked style – see Exercise 113.

LIGHT OPERA SOCIETY,
Village Hall,
Your town.

5th September, (this year)

The next Committee Meeting of the Light Opera Society will be held in the lounge of the Village Hall at 7.00 p.m. on 14th September, (this year). I hope you are able to attend.

AGENDA

1. Apologies for absence.

2. Minutes of the last meeting held on 11th August. Copy enclosed.

3. Matters arising:

    (i) Casting for the next production.
    (ii) Hiring of staging.
    (iii) Insurance of Society costumes.

4. Secretary's report.

5. Treasurer's report.

6. Musical director's report.

7. Costumes for the next production.

8. Any other business.

9. Date, time and place of next meeting.

Jillian Palmer
Honorary Secretary

Enc.

200

Exercise 115

Copy the notice of meeting and agenda on a suitable sheet of paper in any consistent style.

Colpro (1979) Ltd
Enterprise House
Westlands Drive
Your Town

Tele 21217

14 March (this year)

The next meeting of the Employee/Management liaison Committee will be held in the works canteen at 9.30 am on 22 March (this year). If you are unable to attend will you please inform your deputy?

AGENDA

1 Apologies for absence
2 Minutes of the last meeting held on 14 February (this year)
3 Matters arising:
   (a) Bonding on the SP477 units
   (b) Monitoring of trainees' progress
4 Report of Employees' Working Party Chairman
5 Report of Management Working Party Chairman
6 Sales commission
7 O & M
8 In-service training – joint programme
9 Any other business
10 Date, time and place of next meeting

Exercise 116
Type this chairman's agenda on a suitable sheet of paper – see page 197 for instructions. This agenda is linked to that on page 199.

```
AGENDA

1  Apologies for absence      Mr Wilson is on holiday

2  Minutes                    Copies circulated

3  Matters arising

   (i)    Casting for next    Mrs Andrews to report
          production
   (ii)   Hiring of staging   Mr Jenkins to report
   (iii)  Insurance of        Chairman to report on findings
          costumes

4  Secretary's report         Miss Palmer

5  Treasurer's report         Mr Jenkins

6  Musical director's report  Mrs Andrews

7  Costumes for next          Mr Jenkins
   production

8  Any other business         Advertising
                              Printing

9  Date, time and place of    Should be the second Tuesday
   next meeting               in the month.  Village Hall
                              lounge is available
```

202

Exercise 117

Type this chairman's agenda on a suitable sheet of paper. The exercise is linked to that on page 200.

AGENDA

1 Apologies — Mr Wakeman; Mr Roy Burns attending his first meeting as deputy

2 Minutes — Copies available

3 Matters arising
   (a) Bonding on SP477 units — Mr Clay to report
   (b) Monitoring of trainees' progress — Mrs Yates to report for the sub-committee

4 EWP Chairman's report — Mr A'Court

5 MWP Chairman's report — Mr Field

6 Sales commission — Possibility of commission to employees who sell — Mr Bullows

7 O & M — Possibility of joint study — Mr Rough

8 In-service training — Chairman to table paper joint programme

9 Any other business — None — so far

10 Next meeting — Suggested 16 April — usual place

17.4 AGENDA FOR AN ANNUAL GENERAL MEETING

The agenda for an Annual General Meeting (AGM) differs from an ordinary agenda in two ways. Copies are sent to all members of the organisation and not just to committee members and the nature of the business is different. Any additional information extra to that given in the agenda may be set out at its foot. The example below is typical. Type it on a suitable sheet of paper. This agenda below is linked to the exercises on pages 198 and 207.

Example 41

UNION SPORTS AND SOCIAL CLUB

NOTICE OF ANNUAL GENERAL MEETING

Notice is hereby given that the Seventeenth Annual General Meeting of the Union Sports and Social Club will be held at its premises on Thursday, 28 April (this year), at 8.00 pm to transact the following business:-

1   To receive and consider the Accounts for the year (last year) with the Auditors' Report thereon.

2   To adopt the Report for the Chairman for that year.

3   To declare the election or re-election, as the case may be, of Officers and Members of the General Committee.

4   Any other business.

V Robinson
Honorary Secretary
Parklands Avenue
20 March (this year)

NOTES

1   Nominations for Officers and General Committee will be welcomed by the Secretary.

2   The Auditors, Messrs Pinner, Darlington & Co have expressed their willingness to remain in office.

204

Exercise 118

Type this notice of an Annual General Meeting on a suitable sheet of paper. Note the use of capital letters.

COLPRO (1979) PLC

NOTICE OF ANNUAL GENERAL MEETING

NOTICE IS HEREBY GIVEN that the annual general meeting of Colpro (1979) plc will be held at the Imperial Hotel, Park Street, (Your town) at 11.30 am on (day) 12 July (this year) for the following purposes:

As ordinary business:-

1 To receive and adopt the accounts for the 52 weeks ended 6 March (this year) and the reports of the directors and the auditors thereon.

2 To declare a final dividend on the ordinary shares.

3 To re-elect as directors

   (i)   Mr R A Eddison
   (ii) Mr I A Kilvington

4 To re-appoint the auditors and to authorise the directors to fix their remuneration.

As special business:-

5 To consider and, if thought fit, pass the following special resolution:

   "That the directors are hereby empowered for the period from the passing of this resolution until the conclusion of the annual general meeting of the company to be held (next year) to allot equity securities (as defined by Section 16 (i) of the Companies Act (1980) of the company pursuant to the authority conferred on them by resolution of the company passed (last year)".

By order of the Board

S A Piper
Secretary
Tower House
23 June (this year)

Notes

1 Holders of ordinary shares, who alone are entitled to attend and vote at the annual general meeting, are entitled to appoint one or more proxies to attend and, on a poll, vote instead of them.

2 A proxy need not be a member of the company.

Exercise 119

Type this agenda for an Annual General Meeting on a suitable sheet of paper.

INTERNATIONAL METAL PLC

NOTICE OF AGM ← in full please

NOTICE IS HEREBY GIVEN tht t AGM of International Metal PLC wl be held at t Carlton Hotel, Denmark St London on (day) 19 August (this year), f t follg purposes;

1 To consider + adopt t Report of t Directors + t a/cs f t 52 wks ended May 2 (this yr)

2 To declare a dividend

3 To re-elect t follg directors
   Mr B G Fielding
   Mr D H Thorne
   Mr J Walker

4 To re-appoint Taylor, Wilkinson + Co as auditors + t authorise t Board t fix their remuneration

By order of the Board
J M Bryant
Secretary
Canberra House
Canberra Road
(Your town)

21 July (this year)

NOTE
The annual report + a/cs are sent t all shareholders + holders of First Mortgage Debenture Stock, but only ordinary shareholders are entitled t vote or t be represented at t annual general meeting

17.5 **MINUTES**

Minutes are a written record of the events which took place at a meeting. They are usually produced by the secretary or a special minutes secretary – often in consultation with the chairman. Minutes may be kept in a special minute book – handwritten or typed.

When producing minutes, write them in the third person and in the past tense, e.g. 'Mr Rawlinson reported that at a meeting held . . .'. Minutes should accurately reflect the tone of a meeting and balance fairly any points of debate. If formal resolutions are tabled, amended and passed or rejected the minutes should state the proposer and seconder and the resulting decision. The exact wording of formal propositions and amendments should be faithfully recorded. If votes are taken the number of votes cast either way may be recorded. A draft set of minutes is sometimes produced by the person responsible, working with the chairman of the meeting prior to their final production. Minutes should be produced in the order of events at the meeting – and this might not be the order tabled on the agenda. For various reasons it might be decided to change the tabled order and the minutes should reflect this.

Any suitable size of paper may be used for the production of minutes though A4 will normally be used. The opening statement should give the nature, date, time and place of the meeting and it should be followed by a list of those present – usually starting with the officials and then listing, often in alphabetical order, those present. The rest of the items should be listed in the order they were introduced at the meeting and the producer should balance brevity with clarity. The headings should be typed as side/ marginal headings while the general style may be blocked or indented (i.e. centred main/subheading and indented paragraphs). Use single line spacing with a blank line between paragraphs. Should continuation sheets be necessary number the pages in any consistent style as for numbering general material (see page 214). At the foot of the last sheet it is usual to leave space for the chairman to sign the minutes. It is usual to date the signature. Any amendments/alterations to the tabled minutes should be recorded and a reference made to the fact in the next set of minutes to be produced.

For full details relating to the conduct of and preparation for meetings together with the terms used at meetings see my *Mastering Office Practice*, pages 197–208.

The minutes in Exercises 120–122 are fairly typical – bearing in mind the constraints of the page size on which they are produced.

Exercise 120

Copy these minutes, presented in the blocked style, on a sheet of A4 paper.

UNION SPORTS AND SOCIAL CLUB

Meeting No 203

Minutes of the General Committee of the Union Sports and Social Club held in the Committee Room at the centre on Thursday 15 July (this year).

Present:	Mr A Macefield (Chairman) Miss V Robinson (Secretary) Mrs B Morris (Minutes Secretary) Mr R Stean (Treasurer) Miss P Andrews Mr D Dando Miss M Newey
Apologies	Mr Green and Mrs Russon - on holiday.
Minutes	The minutes of the last meeting held on 19 June were read and duly signed by the chairman as being a true record.
Matters arising	Mr Stean reported that the insurers had met the fire damage claim in full.
Secretary's report	Miss Robinson said that she had received a letter of thanks from the Blind School for the donation following the sponsored run organised by the Union.
Treasurer's report	Mr Stean expressed concern at the number of unpaid subscriptions. He was asked to produce a list of offending members for the next meeting.
Cricket captain's report	Mr Dando reported that the 1st XI had reached the final of the KO which would be played at home on 29 July.
Any other business	Miss Andrews said that fresh supplies of tennis equipment was now available at discount rates. All profits from sales would go to Union funds.
Next meeting	It was agreed to hold the next meeting in the Committee Room on 21 August at 1900 hrs.

Chairman

Date

208

Exercise 121

Copy these minutes (produced here in the indented style) on a sheet of A4 paper.

LIGHT OPERA SOCIETY

Meeting No 108

Meeting of the Committee of the Light Opera Society held in the Village Hall on 10 February (this year).

Present: Mr C Dunn (Chairman)
Miss J Palmer (Secretary)
Mr P Jenkins (Treasurer)
Mrs M Andrews (Musical Director)
Miss V Turner
Mr M Wilson

Apologies — Apologies were received from Miss B Nevil and Mrs W Roberts.

Minutes — The minutes of the last meeting which was held on 11 January having previously been circulated were taken as read.

Matters arising — Miss Turner reported that the programmes for the Easter production were now available for sale.

Secretary's report — Miss Palmer reported that she had received five new applications to join. She had arranged, with Mrs Andrews, for the applicants to be tested.

Treasurer's report — Mr Jenkins reported that takings for the Easter production were well up on last year. He said that the Society should exceed its profit target by a long way.

Any other business — Mr Wilson asked about the possibility of forming a small orchestra to save the expense of hiring musicians for productions. A sub-committee of the Chairman, Secretary, Musical Director and Mr Wilson was set up to look into the matter.

Next meeting — It was agreed to leave the arranging of the next meeting to the Secretary and Chairman.

Chairman ....

Date ....

Exercise 122

Set out this set of minutes correctly (in any consistent style) on a sheet of A4 paper.

DRAMA SOCIETY

Meeting No 82

Minutes of the Drama Society Committee held in the Union Sports Centre Committee Room on 4 October (this year)

Present: Miss K Perry (Chairman) Mr V Hughes (Hon Sec) Mrs A Fellows (Director) Miss C Downes (Treasurer) Mr R Knight, Mrs P Lawson, Mr I Stokes, Miss I Weaver

Apologies: Apologies were received from Mrs O Trager

Minutes: Mrs Lawson pointed out that she had been at the previous meeting but was not listed as being present. The secretary apologised and the amended minutes were duly signed.

Matters arising: The Director reported that she had managed to obtain sufficient copies of "The Spy from The Ministry" for the next production to be rehearsed without further purchases. The Chairman thanked her for her efforts which had saved a lot of money.

Correspondence: The secretary reported that she had received a letter from the Westacre Society enquiring about the use of the Society's portable staging. It was agreed to loan it free of charge.

Treasurer's report: The treasurer reported that she had received a donation from Mrs B Vernon to cover the costumes for the next production. The secretary was asked to write and thank her for her generous donation.

AOB Miss Weaver asked who would be responsible for the lighting now that Mr V Thomas had left the area. Members were asked to give the matter thought before the next meeting.

Next meeting: It was agreed to leave details to the chairman & secretary.

Chairman

Date

ACCOUNTS

Accounts are used to present financial information and most clubs, societies and companies produce them at least annually. Some clubs and societies present their accounts on a double entry basis (horizontally). This style is now considered 'old fashioned' and the vertical style of presentation is more usual.

18.1 ACCOUNTS PRESENTED VERTICALLY

The modern trend is to present accounts vertically in columns as in Example 42. Associated items are grouped together and totalled separately.

To type vertical accounts treat them as columns in tabular work and total the items as you would money in columns. Sometimes the previous year's figures are listed in a separate column for comparative purposes.

Example 42
Copy the vertical account below on to a sheet of A4 paper.

INDUSTRIAL EQUIPMENT PLC

Balance sheet as at 31 December (last year)

	Last Year £m	Previous Year £m
Fixed assets	650.2	650.2
Special equipment	95.8	80.0
Trade investments	12.2	14.0
Net current assets	85.6	80.4
	843.8	824.6
Financed by		
Share capital	450.0	425.0
Reserves	110.0	95.0
	560.0	520.0
Loan stock	83.8	83.8
Other loan stock	150.0	170.0
Finance leasing liability	50.0	50.8
	843.8	824.6

Exercise 123
Type this balance sheet on a sheet of A4 paper.

COLPRO (1979) PLC

Balance sheet as at 6 March (last year)

	Last Year £m	Previous Year £m
Capital employed		
Ordinary shares	224.9	204.9
Reserves	151.6	140.0
	376.5	344.9
Loan capital	95.0	90.0
Deferred taxation	5.2	4.0
	476.7	438.9
Assets employed		
Stock	87.5	80.5
Debtors	102.1	90.6
Cash receivable	120.0	100.0
	309.6	271.1
Borrowings	10.4	11.0
Creditors	150.6	140.2
Taxation payable	8.6	7.8
Dividends payable	9.2	8.4
	178.8	167.4
Net current assets	130.7	113.7
Land, buildings, plant and equipment	275.6	260.2
Long-term assets	70.4	65.0
Fixed assets	346.0	325.2
Assets employed	476.7	438.9

Exercise 124

Type the balance sheet on a sheet of A4 paper.

UNION SPORTS AND SOCIAL CLUB BALANCE SHEET
as at 31 December (last year)

	Last year		Previous year
General Fund (Note 1)		23 491	24 416
Special Fund		874	624
		24 365	25040
Assets and Liabilities			
Fixed Assets (Note 2)		45 703	28 351
Current Assets			
Stock at cost	2395		2510
Debtors	1280		1066
Sundry Investments	10		10
Savings accounts	—		8535
Cash and Bank Balances	1274		2539
	4959		14660
Current Liabilities			
Creditors	9586		7678
Unsecured Loans (Note 3)	1100		1150
Bank overdraft	7468		—
	18154	13235	8828	5832
		32468		34183
Deferred Liabilities			
Loans from Members	3676		3676
Loans from Sporting Bodies	50		100
Unsecured Loans (Note 3)	4377	8103	5367	9143
		24365		25040

CONTINUATION SHEETS IN GENERAL MATERIAL

19.1 GENERAL MATERIAL

If material has to be produced on more than one sheet of paper it must be continued on sheets of paper the same size, colour and quality as the first sheet and using the same margins, line spacing and style as the first sheet (blocked or indented, etc.).

When work has to be typed on the back of the first page, the left and right margins should be reversed and the paper adjusted so that the lines of type are on top of each other.

Catchwords - words which lead the eye from one page to another - may be typed (with a short row of dots before or after), in any consistent position below the last line of type. The catchwords usually used are: Continued (or any abbreviation of the word), /Over, /over, or PTO (P.T.O.). Sometimes the first 2 or 3 words from the following page are typed, with a short row of full stops before or after them.

Pages should be numbered within the top margin or within the bottom margin. Some examination authorities will accept the page numbers typed consistently at the left margin. Others prefer page numbers to be typed at the left or right margins when using the blocked style or in the centre of the typing line when using the indented style.

Margins should be at least 25 mm (1 in) top and bottom of the page and you should carry over at least a complete line (preferably at least 2 complete lines) of a paragraph.

Word processing programs will automatically indicate page breaks, number sheets and head documents in a variety of fashions. Consult your manual to see what your program offers - look under *pagination*. The available 'features' vary according to the program used, as does the mode of operation.

Exercise 125
Type this article on sheets of A4 paper in double line spacing. Use any consistent style. Head the article FASHION – LITERALLY. Some words have been abbreviated – type them in full (see page 178).

Shakespeare once wrote a poem abt t world beg a stage & men & women beg players – all playing many parts in t course of their lives. He went on to describe some of t parts played. What he forgot to mention was tht ea part was played agnst a diffnt scenery & tht just as people change during their lives, no two ages are the same. It would be interesting to see how t great man would write today against t modern background.

Many of Shakespeare's greatest plays were written against a historical background but one of today's fashions is to write abt t future. While in a sense he wrote of a fantasy world when he wrote A Midsummer Night's Dream he cd never hv dreamed of t worlds envisaged by mny writers of serious & not so serious material today.

Wh seems to happen in literary circles is tht writers seek to achieve fame & fortune (if not emotional release) by adoptg one of a number of 'ploys'. They may seek to reform wh they perceive to be a number of 'faults' or undesirable trends in society by highlightg wh they see as beg t worst aspects – they comment on society. Others seek to shock t reader either by t use of forceful language or graphic descriptns of t horrific or t unspeakable – although it cd be argued th lttle of t latter remains in modern society. There are also t old faithfuls in t 'historical comment' angle or t 'predictns of t future'.

One current literary fashion, wh past generations cd not follow, bec t technology was not there, is th of writg f t screen. Today's fashionable writers often take great pains to ensure that whatever they write can be made into a stage play or a film f showing on either t small screen (TV) or t large screen (cinema) – or better still on both. While modern producers can hire writers to adapt earlier works f t screen or stage one can only guess at t outcome had t original author had some exposure to modern developments.

Yet another 'modern fashion' is f writers to get together to produce works as a team - t idea seeming to be th as one runs out of ideas another can take over & provide t stimulus when t next writer, in turn, runs out of ideas. This 'ploy' has great commercial value whn a film or TV series can be made out of a particular work. It is not unknown for public demand to perpetuate t 'works' of favourite authors after their death. Ghost writers are hired to write in t same style & to give t impression that nothing has changed.

No doubt stimulated by t needs of publishers to maximise their profits there is an increasing fashion f authors to write f t universal market. While there can be no doubt th t writings of some great figs of t past did translate (& relate in a meaningful fashion) to other languages it is equally true that some did not 'travel' very well. Modern writers find it profitable to be aware of t universal market.

Just as t stage scenery changes fr generatn to generation so does t 'mode of delivery'. One aspect of modern writing is t rarity of writers of, or in, verse. Returning to t 'great man' it is worth commenting on how many of his works were written in verse. Within recent times it was fashionable to write, & read, poetry yet today t emphasis tends to be purely on t narrative - with another eye on t film no doubt!

What wl be interesting will be to see how new technology affects writing fashions. Will t fashion become th of writing short episodes f t 'soap opera' just as some writers of music wrote f t size of record their works were to be recorded on? What impact will new technology hv on writers? It is often forgotten th t majority of t great literary works were written w quills & t very act of writing must have been extremely difficult, apart from being very slow. One thing is for sure; fashions will change & authors will continue to exploit every means at their disposal.

19.2 CHAIRMAN'S REPORTS

A chairman's report comments on the work and finance of an institution and usually accompanies the financial statement published for discussion at the Annual General Meeting. Reports can be typed in any consistent style on suitable paper, using continuation sheets if necessary.

Exercise 126
Type this Chairman's Report on sheets of A4 paper using single line spacing for the numbered section (leaving a blank line between each numbered item) and double line spacing for the rest. Head the first sheet: UNION SPORTS AND SOCIAL CLUB. Use blocked or indented paragraphs.

CHAIRMAN'S REPORT

The year ended 31 December (last year) saw great changes in the facilities of the Club. The following work was undertaken and completed:-

1   Central heating has been installed throughout the Club.

2   The showers have been replaced by an electric system.

3   The walls in the shower area have been retiled.

4   The floors of the changing room, shower area and the corridor have been retiled.

5   The lounge has been refurbished and redecorated. The windows have been replaced by double glazing.

6   The entrance hall and toilets have been redecorated.

7   The snooker tables have been re-covered.

8   The kitchen has been redecorated and more modern equipment has been installed.

9   The tennis courts have been resurfaced.

As you will see, from the balance sheet, these improvements have cost a great deal of money and to meet the cost the Club has had to agree to an overdraft with the bank. It is felt, by the treasurer, that this debt could be paid off by (4 years time) but whether this can be achieved depends upon you, the members. Your increased support is urgently needed, not only that of the 'regulars' but also by an increase in the attendance of the 'occasionals' and, hopefully, that some members who at present never use the Club will start to do so. Now that all the changes have been completed it really is a pleasure to spend an evening at the Club - so please give all the support you can. (Paragraph) As you will see, in the Newsletter, a change in the date and format of the Union Sports and Social Club Open Day is to be made. There will be no Dinner this year and the next Dinner will take place in March (next year). We hope to make a day of it rather than just a Dinner in the evening. The facilities of the Club will be open during the day and we hope to encourage people not currently associated with the Club to attend and take an active part. (Paragaraph) I have great pleasure in record- ing another very successful year on our various fields of play. The football section now fields 5 teams regularly while the hockey section goes from strength to strength; both 1st and 2nd teams won their leagues. Tennis and cricket continue to flourish and next year the latter hopes to play in 3 leagues. The bowls section is developing several good players while the indoor activities have a thriving membership. (Paragraph) Our recent decision to open the Club for out- siders to hold meetings is proving successful and will, hope- fully, bring an increase in the sporting membership. (Paragraph) Clearly a Club of this nature cannot work without a great deal of hard work and effort. I would like to pay my tribute to the dedication shown by your officers during this period of change. Without their tireless efforts the Club would not be in its current position. As indicated earlier, the Club now needs your support to clear its debts. Your officers have given a splendid example and deserve your fullest support. (Paragraph) Finally I would like to offer thanks, on your behalf, to our paid staff for all their sterl- ing work both on and off the field.

N B Stokes
Chairman

Exercise 127
Type this Chairman's Statement on suitable sheets of paper – use any style.
COLPRO (1979) PLC

Chairman's Statement

(Last year) was a year of great progress and the improvement in net profit before taxation was the highest achieved since we set the business on its present course. It is of great credit to our managers and staff that, despite the economic climate, they should have established new records for the Company. This must encourage them and provide the necessary confidence for pursuing, consistently, our policies of concentrated effort and investment. (Paragraph) Compared with (previous year) sales were up from 1215 m to 1323 m, an increase of 8.8% with profit before taxation at 75.8 m, 29.3% ahead of the previous year. Profitability at the pre-tax level benefited from higher investment income, of which 51.2 m arose from the Rights Issue and from holding the interest payable figure just below that of (last year). (Paragraph) It was important to achieve sales growth in (last year) and those responsible for marketing and selling the Company's products clearly struck the right balance between sales volume and the protection of sales margins. In this they were greatly assisted by the continuing improvement in labour productivity – which was reflected in the 'value for money' offered to our customers who, as always, are concerned with price and quality. (Paragraph) The main change in the Balance Sheet results from the (last year) Rights Issue which was a great success. I applaud the way our shareholders responded to the Issue and the way they gave practical assistance to the Board. The Rights Issue will enable the Company to develop the business at home and overseas at a faster rate than would otherwise have been possible. It has permanently increased the Company's capital and investment income. These funds have put the Company in a position to invest in the development of the business by increased trade and by, as is opportune, acquisition. We are currently actively engaged in reviewing opportunities for the expansion of the Company along these lines. (Paragraph) Our first priority is the growth of the Company's existing business and we have strengthened our planning systems to this end. All managers of operating units should regard the future development and growth of that unit as one of his/her key tasks. The planning from the bottom up must also be matched by planning from the top down to ensure that the Company makes the most of its opportunities. The key role of acquisitions is to bring about strategic shifts in our products or the geographical balance of the Company. (Paragraph) Returning to results round the world, all regions, except Europe, increased their trading profits over the previous year. Results from the American continent are encouraging with all sections increasing their profits and volume sales. The Canadian section showed large gains in market share and profitability. The Australian division, despite a very difficult business environment, showed record sales while the New Zealand section also achieved the highest level of profitability in its history. Colpro Nigeria achieved a significant increase in sales and profits while the Indian division's profits were marginally above budget. (Paragraph) This brief review of our world trade gives me the confidence to predict that the coming year will be even better for the Company. The Company is making real progress and this progress is due to teamwork. At a time when jobs in the manufacturing industries throughout the world are declining it is essential that we achieve maximum output from our labour force to lower unit costs. The introduction of new technology can only be fully effective if all concerned are aware of its potential both in terms of productivity but also in working conditions and job/career aspirations. The prime duty of any Company faced with these fundamental changes in the structure and nature of employment must be to maintain its competitive ability. If it fails in this area it puts yet more jobs at risk. (Paragraph) MEMBERSHIP OF THE BOARD (Paragraph) A couple of Board changes took place during the year under review. Mr Eric Teddington has retired after 10 years service and I wish him well. His astute comments will be missed. He is replaced by Mr Patrick Durnell who served as a non-executive director for 5 years and who will, I am sure, maintain the strength of the Board to whom I offer my sincere thanks.

Henry Squires
Chairman

MANUSCRIPT PREPARATION

You may be called upon to type a *thesis* for a student or a *typescript* (a manuscript typed for a printer). The approach, in either case, is very similar but before attempting the work you should find out if there are any special constraints such as width of printing line, page size and 'house style' of presentation. The following applies to material produced on a typewriter. Users of word processors must follow the program for their particular machine, but what follows still relates to them. The particular advantages of word processors in manuscript preparation are: the ease with which material can be edited on the VDU, the speed at which specific typographical errors can be corrected (if a word has consistently been mis-spelt the machine can be instructed to search for it and correct it each time it occurs), the ease of altering formats without the need to retype, the help given when indexing (the machine can be instructed to search for words and indicate where they are to be found) and the fact that you can print as many copies of the text as you require.

Example 43
Type the following as though preparing it for a printer or as a thesis.
Read through it first and follow the instructions included.

1 Use a suitable size of paper. The usual size is A4 (210 x
   297 mm) although some manuscripts are produced on other
   paper sizes. Use good quality paper because it will be
   subjected to a lot of handling. Poor quality paper soon
   becomes unusable.

2 Produce the material in double line spacing on one side of
   the page only using ample margins. The editor (in the
   case of a typescript in particular) needs space in which
   to edit the text and mark it up for the printer. Most
   printers require the typeface to be a consistent width (in
   other words they do not like proportional spacing) and
   they like each page to contain the same number of lines of
   type. Even if parts of the text are to be printed in
   single line spacing (extracts or notes for example) they
   must be produced in double line spacing and a note made in
   the margin. Some printers make an extra charge for
   working on typescripts produced in single line spacing.

3 Margins should be a minimum of 25 mm (1 in) at the head,
   foot and right of the page and 38 mm (1½ in) at the left.
   If the material is a manuscript/thesis which is to be
   bound the left margin, also known as a <u>stitching margin</u>,
   may need to be slightly wider. The copy-editor and the
   printer's estimator need the wide left margin for their
   notes. The wide margins in general help to protect the
   typescript.

4 The style of layout should be consistent - blocked or
   centred headings and indented paragraphs. Check to see if
   a particular style is required.

5 Footnotes should be produced as for a printer when producing typescripts while those in a thesis should be produced
   as for a typist.

6 Number the <u>folios</u> (pages) in a consistent position. Some
   printers require the numbers to be typed in the top right-
   hand corner only, so check. While chapters may also be
   numbered printers will refer to folio numbers only when

corresponding and not to chapter numbers. It is usual to indicate the number of folios in the typescript on the front cover.

7   Last-minute alterations may be written in black ink but if they are substantial they should be typed on separate full-sized sheets of paper and numbered accordingly (eg 123a, 123b).

8   Avoid using pins or staples which are likely to tear off and take words with them or paper clips which can fall out or stick to other sheets. Use transparent tape on the back of folios only (if it is used on the front it is often impossible to write on).

9   Keep a copy of the typescript. Send the original. Some typists take one or more carbon copies as they produce the original but this can take time. An expensive option is to photocopy. (Word processors score heavily here.)

10 Protect with heavy duty card before posting material.

20.1 BOOK STRUCTURE

The information given on the previous pages relates to both typescripts and theses, but the preparation of typescripts poses additional problems, as detailed below. As an additional exercise produce the text shown in Example 44 as though you were producing a typescript on sheets of A4 paper. Head it: BOOK STRUCTURE.

224

Example 44

Books usually consist of 3 elements: the preliminary pages (also known as <u>prelims</u>, the text and the index (known as <u>the endmatter</u>).

<u>Preliminary pages</u> are usually numbered separately in small Roman numerals, a convention which allows for last-minute alterations without affecting the numbering of pages in the main text. The preliminary pages might contain such information as:-

<u>The half-title</u> - a page giving the title of the book only. This is the first page in a book and it always appears as a right-hand page, protecting the rest of the book.

<u>The half-title verso</u> - a page which lists any other books produced by the author or any other books in the series.

<u>The copyright page</u> on which details of the author and other legal requirements are printed.

<u>The contents</u> - which may take up several pages and include a list of diagrams/illustrations, chapter headings and sections.

<u>A foreword</u> - a statement by an outsider as to the book's merit and/or a <u>preface</u>, an introduction to it by the author(s).

THE TEXT

The text is usually produced in parts or chapters. When producing typescripts check to see what 'house style' is used for the presentation of main and sub-headings. Some publishers number the headings with the weight of typeface to be used while others give them letters. Leave space for the insertion of illustrations/diagrams and number them - the numbers should correspond with those on the diagrams etc.

THE INDEX

The index, or endmatter, may consist purely of the index but it may also include any appendices.

The production of an index is usually the responsibility of the author. Apart from using a word processor the most practical way of producing an index is to use a series of cards of a suitable size (A5 or A6). To produce an index using cards:

1 Mark each card with a letter of the alphabet.

2 Work through the text and list the items you want to index on the appropriate card(s). Most items will require a cross-reference. For example: Manuscript abbreviations may be also be listed under Abbreviations - Manuscript.

3 When the whole text has been listed on the cards type the information on suitable sheets of paper, usually A4, in alphabetical order as for the preparation of typescripts.

4 Check each entry against the text.

PROOF READING

Before a book is published the proofs set by the printer have to be read and all errors noted using correction signs. It is advisable to have one person read through the typescript while another checks the proofs for errors and omissions. Repeat the process reversing the roles. Always check, in particular, any cross-references.

COPYRIGHT MATERIAL

It is illegal to reproduce material which is copyright without permission. Sometimes the permission will be given free of charge, provided the source is acknowledged, while at others a charge is made. In the UK the period of copyright extends until 50 years after the author's death, or, if the work is published after the author's death, until 50 years after publication.

20.2 **PLAYS**

There are several conventions used when typing plays but what follows is
universally acceptable. Plays are usually typed on good quality A4 paper
and consist of 4 elements: *the title page, the setting and the scenes, the
characters* and *the play itself.*

Example 45
Copy the information which follows as though you were preparing a typescript on A4 paper. Head it: TYPING PLAYS.

THE TITLE PAGE

The title page gives the name of the play and the author.
This information is usually typed centrally on the page with
the name of the play followed by the name of the author. The
page has the same function as the title page of a book.

THE SETTING AND THE SCENES

This (second) page gives the setting or synopsis of the play
together with a list of the scenes. The style of this page
should follow that used for the title page.

THE CHARACTERS

The characters in the play are listed on the third page and
they may appear in alphabetical order or in the order in which
they appear in the play. If the play is in production the
names of the people playing the characters are displayed with
the characters.

THE PLAY ITSELF

The play itself is typed using a wide left margin for the
names of the characters which are typed as side headings. The
first page of the play proper usually has a <u>dropped heading</u>,
to leave space, usually 75 mm (3 in), for a plan of the scene
to be sketched in later. <u>Stage directions</u> are typed in the
body of the page and are often underscored in red or have a
red ink line drawn under them to make them stand out. The
style of presentation may be blocked or indented consistently.
Continuation pages should be numbered as for continuous
material.

20.3 SINGLE ACTORS' PARTS

When a play goes into production single actors' parts are often produced
to save individuals carrying a copy of the whole play all the time.

Example 46
Type the information which follows as though you were producing a
manuscript on A4 paper. Head it: SINGLE ACTORS' PARTS.

It is usual to produce single actors' parts on sheets of good
quality A5 (210 x 148 mm) bond paper. Individual actors do
not need to see all the play, only their own parts. To help
them to understand when it is their turn to say/do something
cue lines are given.

Produce single actors' parts in single line spacing with
narrow margins of 13 mm ($\frac{1}{2}$ in) each side of the page. Type
the name of the character at the head of each sheet which may
be produced, consistently, in the blocked or the indented
style. The cue words are preceded by ellipses (a series of 3
spaced or 3 unspaced full stops which indicate that material
has been omitted) and are the last words spoken before the
actor has to say or do something. They cue, or prompt, the
actor. The cue words may be typed at the left margin or be
justified to the right margin.

Stage directions are usually underscored in red or have red
lines ruled under them.

The words to be spoken by the actor are often typed in double
line spacing using 10 pitch type for ease of reading.

20.4 TAILPIECE

Sometimes an ornamental combination of characters is produced at the
end of an article, chapter or section of a book. The usual combinations are
made using hyphens and 'o' keys as below. Practise producing them on
suitable sheets of paper.

```
   --ooOoo--        --o-O-o--         ooooo
                                       ooo
                                        o
```

20.5 POETRY

When typing poems use suitable sheets of paper and equal margins or a left margin which is wider than the right. Top and bottom margins should be roughly equal. Basically, poems are of 3 styles:

    those with every line rhyming;
    those with alternate lines rhyming;
    those with no lines rhyming.

The style of layout depends on the style of the poem.

Every line or no lines rhyming
In poems where every line rhymes or no lines rhyme, all lines start at the left margin.

Alternate lines rhyme
Where alternate lines rhyme in a poem the alternate lines should begin 2 spaces in from the left margin.

If a poem has a line, or lines, which are too wide to fit the page the 'extra' words should be typed above or below the lines to which they refer. The term *hook-in* is used to describe this process.

Exercise 128

Type the poems which follow on suitable sheets of paper following the
directions given in section 20.5. In the first poem every line rhymes while
in the second alternate lines rhyme. In the other examples no lines rhyme.

Poem 1

THE LINCOLNSHIRE POACHER

When I was bound apprentice, in famous Lincolnshire,
Full well I served my master for more than seven year,
Till I took up to poaching, as you shall quickly hear:
Oh, 'tis my delight on a shining night, in the season
                                              of the year.

                                                    Anonymous

Poem 2

BADGER

We often watch the ducks at play
    Amid the reeds and grasses,
Or on the pools which look so grey,
    Except when sunlight flashes.

We take our son, who thinks it fun
    To feed them by the water,
He likes to see the way they come
    From every poolside quarter.

Poem 3

BRIDGNORTH
The winding road runs down the hill
To reach the river bank,
And on the right, below a bluff
The waiting churchyard stands.

The water glints and takes the eye
Towards the sandstone bridge,
And upwards climbs the winding road
Towards the Telford church.

From hill to hill the vista lies,
The river and its plain,
And on the cliff, in silhouette,
The town of Bridgnorth stands.

Poem 4

1

I think, I feel, I now exist
Some human form I take,
But whence came I; where shall I go
When earth my body takes?

There must have been a time before,
When other shape I took
But who, or what, decreed that I
This present form should take?

What purpose lies behind this Time
When my whole conscious is?
What will become of all I do
When my life span is through?

Am I a part of some Great Plan
Or does my present state
Belong to other — minor point
To which no thing relates?

The Universal clock moves on,
The earth in space exists
A speck of dust around a sun
Where my whole being is.

COPYING AND DUPLICATING

Copies of typed material are often required for the purpose of records. The quickest way to take up to 6 copies of a document is to take carbon copies - see page 40. Users of memory typewriters and word processors can print as many copies as they require and each will be of identical quality; indeed, some firms use such machines to produce the personalised letter - see page 60.

The easiest way of reproducing a copy of an original document is to photocopy it. If you decide to type a copy of an original document the most accurate way is to get another person to check your copy as you read the original.

21.1 DUPLICATING

The most commonly used methods of duplicating typed material are spirit, ink and offset litho. The method chosen will depend on the available equipment and often there is no choice - you use that which is available. If there is a choice the factors to be taken into account will be: the number of copies required, the use of colour and the use of illustrations. There is not a great deal to choose between them in terms of cost per copy, and the ease of use is often a personal preference rather than an actuality.

Spirit duplicating

If up to 200 copies of a document are required and if a range of colours is a consideration the choice will be spirit duplicating. The process involves the use of master sheets, hectographic carbons and a duplicator.

To produce a master on a typewriter:

1. Place a sheet of hectographic carbon of a suitable colour on the desk top *carbon side up*. There is usually a choice of 6 colours.

2. Place a master sheet, shiny side downwards, on top of the carbon. The master sheets are sheets which have been coated with china clay.

3. Put the carbon and master sheet into your typewriter so that the back of the master is towards you as you type. Treat the master as you would an ordinary sheet of paper and set suitable margins leaving at least 25 mm (1 in) top and bottom.

4. If the machine is a manual one type with a firm, even touch and take care when typing the 'o' key in particular so that you do not cut holes in the master. If the machine is an electric or electronic model set the impact setting to 'high'. It is advisable, if there is a choice of type faces, to use a sharp face and not a broad, flat one.

5. If you make a mistake you must correct it on the reverse of the master. There are 4 alternatives:

   (a) Paint over the error using an appropriate correcting fluid; your supplier can advise.

   (b) Scrape the carbon off the master using a sharp blade.

   (c) Use a special putty rubber to erase the error. An ordinary eraser will cause the carbon to smudge.

   (d) Type the correction on a piece of master paper and stick it over the error. This is advisable if the error is a large one.

   If you opt for one of the first 3 alternatives you should type the correction with a fresh piece of carbon by choice.

Some typewriters can be fitted with a special hectographic carbon ribbon attachment which does away with the need for carbon sheets. If you are using a memory typewriter or a word processor edit your text before producing the master, and avoid the problem of correcting.

Use the same master but different coloured carbons for any required colours and build up the master. Diagrams or drawings may be drawn using a ball-point pen with a master and carbon on a hard, flat surface such as a sheet of glass or metal.

Running off copies

The mode of operation depends on the machine; some are sophisticated electronic machines while others are simple manual machines. Essentially, the process involves fixing the master to the steel drum in the duplicator and passing sheets of duplicating paper through the machine. As each sheet passes through, the spirit (alcohol) used in the machine dissolves a small quantity of carbon from the master and deposits it on the duplicating paper. After a time all the carbon will be exhausted and you will need to make another master.

Masters may be taken off the machine and stored for future use, while additions may be made in the manner previously described. The limiting factors are the amount of carbon on the back of the master and the skill of the duplicating machine operator when running off copies. If too much pressure or spirit is used fewer copies can be run off. Care must be also taken to ensure that copies are run off in a well ventilated room and that a no smoking rule is applied: the alcohol burns readily. As copies leave the machine they are damp but they soon dry out – another reason for sufficient ventilation.

If copies produced on a spirit duplicator are exposed to direct sunlight they tend to fade over a period of time. Some colours, yellow for example, fade more quickly than others, such as black.

Ink duplicating

If 2 or 3 thousand copies of a document are required in one or 2 colours the ink duplicating process should be used. The process involves a waxed skin, the stencil, which is fastened to a backing sheet. Between the skin and the backing sheet there is usually a sheet of double-sided, 'use-once' carbon paper. Essentially, where the waxed skin is punctured by writing, typing or other processes ink from a duplicating machine passes through and duplicating paper is 'printed' with an ink version of the material. Two colours may be used but each will require a separate stencil and either 2 ink duplicators (one for each colour) or the facility to change the ink in the duplicator after washing out the first colour. The usual colours are black and red but for most users only one colour is involved. As for spirit duplicating, the range of duplicating machines available is very wide and at one end of the spectrum is the hand-inked, hand-operated, manual machine while at the other is the fully automatic electronic machine. The operation of the machines vary so consult the relevant handbook.

Ink duplicator masters may be cut on any typewriter and space may be left for the later insertion of diagrams – made using a special stylus. These are available in several sizes.

To prepare ink duplicator stencils on a typewriter:

1. Choose a suitable stencil for your typewriter. This is most important since the use of the wrong type can damage your machine and produce poor copies. Consult your dealer for the most suitable stencils. Manual typewriters and single element machines require different kinds of stencils. Check also that the perforations at the head of the stencil fit your duplicating machine.
2. Use a type face which is clean and sharp. A dirty type face or a broad, flat face will produce poor results.
3. Insert the stencil, carbon and backing sheet into the machine and set margins according to the lines printed on the waxed skin.

4. Put the typewriter on 'stencil'. If this is not possible, remove the ribbon. As you type, the double-sided carbon will enable you to see what you have typed.
5. If the machine is an electric or electronic model and has an impact setting, set it to 'high'. If the machine is a manual, type firmly and deliberately so that a clear impression is cut in the waxed skin – but take care not to type the a, e and o keys in particular too hard. Unless you take care you will cut these letters out of the stencil completely and the copies you run off will contain a lot of black spots.
6. If you make a mistake, wind the stencil slightly out of the machine and insert a ball-point pen or a pencil between the waxed skin and the carbon so that they are separated. Paint out the error on the waxed skin using the appropriate correcting fluid. This fluid is usually pink or white – the former shows up more easily but both are satisfactory. When the fluid is completely dry, remove your pen or pencil and rewind to the typing point before typing the correction and continuing.
7. Before taking a completed stencil out of the typewriter check it carefully. It is advisable to ask another person to read what you have typed as you read the original.

If you are using a memory typewriter or a word processor, edit your text before cutting a stencil. It is advisable to clean the type face after cutting each stencil and certainly before attempting normal typewriting.

After running off copies, the master, which is separated from the backing sheet before running off, can be stored for later use.

Offset litho
Offset litho duplicating enables thousands of copies of material to be run off on a variety of papers in a vast range of colours. The process is used to print newspapers and glossy magazines as well as books and routine documents. The process involves a master plate and an offset duplicator. The plate may be made of paper, plastic or metal and it can be produced in a number of ways.

To produce offset litho plates on a typewriter:

1. Choose a suitable plate. Metal plates, made of flexible aluminium, can be used for a great many copies while paper plates do not permit so many.
2. Use an offset litho ribbon; your supplier will advise. There is a range of colours available.
3. If you are using an electric or electronic machine set the impact setting so that a clear impression is created without the keys pitting the surface of the plate. If you are using a manual machine aim for the same effect – a good impression without pitting.

4. Errors must be corrected with care – greasy finger marks will print! Again, special care must be taken to avoid pitting the plate because this will produce poor copies.
5. Leave space for the later insertion of photographs, illustrations or diagrams.

Once the plate has been prepared it has to be etched (wetted using a special solution provided by the manufacturer), fixed into the machine and copies run off. The etching and fixing is automatic on many machines. Plates can be stored for later use and additions can be made.

Offset litho is the ideal method of duplicating high quality material on a range of materials and in virtually any colour, but there are fewer models available than there are of the simpler spirit and ink duplicators.

21.2 CUTTING AND PASTING

Sometimes a typist may be asked to build up pages from a range of material – typed, hand-drawn, photographs and so on. This may involve cutting out elements and pasting them up on marked sheets before photo-copying, photographing or making into plates for use on one of the processes discussed earlier. If the master sheet is marked up using a light (Cambridge) blue pencil the lines or marks made on it will not show when the material is photocopied or photographed.

The term 'cutting and pasting' also refers to some word processing functions which have the same end result as manual cutting and pasting. Sometimes the term *boiler plating* refers to the process of making up a document from prepared banks of words, phrases and paragraphs in a micro/word processor memory. This process is an 'advanced form' of mail merging – see also page 60.

21.3 FLOPPY DISKS AND CASSETTES

Floppy disks, used for storing information used in word processors and microcomputers, should always be handled with care and be kept in a dust free environment. When not in use they should be kept in the envelope provided and be stored in an appropriate file. Always label disks clearly and fix a protective tag over the slot on master disks so that the possi-bility of removing information accidentally is prevented. Disks should not be allowed to come into contact with electrical or magnetic equipment because both can damage the information stored on them. It is advisable to take copies of each disk so that in the event of failure the information is not lost. The same rules apply to information stored on cassettes.

When entering information into a micro or word processor save it regularly. Any loss of power will result in the loss of information in the process of being handled in a *buffer* or *working memory*, but information stored on a disk or cassette can easily be put back into the machine.

APPENDIX A

THE TABULATOR

Most typewriters have a tabulator device of some kind – the exceptions being some portable machines. A tabulator enables the operator to find predetermined positions when working across a page – or in the case of an operator with a VDU, points on the screen. On some typewriters the tabulator keys are set at fixed, regular intervals so that the operator has, for example, stops at 10, 20, 30 40 and so on across the page. Such a tabulator mechanism is called a *decimal tabublator*. Most typewriters have a tabular mechanism which enables the operator to set tabulator stops (often called *tab stops*) at any desired position. The position and method of operation of the tabulator keys varies from machine to machine and you should consult the manual for your machine before progressing. If you are using a microcomputer with a word processing program you will have to use the command keys as instructed in the manual. There is usually a sequence of commands required to clear/set the tabulator and a key – rather like the tabulator bar or tabulator key on a typewriter – is used to operate the mechanism once it is set.

What you have probably found on your typewriter is that the machine has a key marked 'TAB' (if it has a decimal tabulator it is probably marked 'DECIMAL TAB'), and two other keys marked 'SET' and 'CLEAR'. You might have a tab bar running across the front of the machine above the top row keys with a key marked (–) on one side and a key marked (+) on the other. Again you might find the SET and CLR (for *clear*) on the same rocking switch. If you press the TAB key the carriage (if your machine is a type bar machine) or the head (if the machine is single element) will move across the typing line until it meets a tab key which has been set. If your machine has a VDU, the cursor will jump across the screen.

To clear a tab, press the TAB key and wait until the carriage or head stops. At this point press the (–) or CLR key. Press the tab key again and clear any others as required. On some machines one operation can clear all tab settings in addition to that required to clear individual settings –

see your handbook. *To set a tab*, move the carriage or head to the required position and press the (+) or SET key. Repeat the operation, setting as many tab keys as you require. On some electronic typewriters the setting and clearing of tabs requires the use of command keys – rather like a microcomputer or word processor.

Tabs are useful for finding any required point on a page or VDU in a range of tasks – especially in the production of tables.

Exercise A.1

Practise using the tabulator.

Clear all tab settings.

Set tabs at: 10, 15, 25, 30, 40, 60, 75.

Check the settings and then clear every other one. Check the settings before clearing them all and setting tabs as you require.

To centre a word about the middle of any page Find the middle of the width of the page – measure it and divide its width by 2. If there is an odd number move to the next highest number. Move the printing point to that point. Back-space once for every 2 letters in the word; if there is an odd letter ignore it. Example. To centre *typewriters* back-space ty pe wr it er – and ignore the odd letter 's'. Type *typewriters*.

To centre a line about the middle of any page Find the middle of the width of the page (as above) and move the printing point to that point. Back-space once for every 2 letters and spaces in the line and ignore any odd letter. Example. To centre *Two sheets of paper* back-space Tw ospace sh ee ts spaceo fspace pa pe – and ignore the odd letter 'r'. Type *Two sheets of paper*.

To centre about the middle of the typing line Add the 2 margins together and divide by 2 to find the middle of the typing line. If there is an odd number move to the next highest number. Example: Margins 12–77. $12 + 77 = 89$. $89 \div 2 = 44\frac{1}{2}$. Call it 45. Centre a word or words about this point as described above.

TYPING PAPER

Quality

Typing paper is sold in grades according to its weight and the modern convention is to describe its weight in terms of grams per square metre or g/m^2 for short. Good quality paper weighs 70 g/m^2 and is often described as Bond paper. Thin typing paper is often called Bank paper and this weighs 45 g/m^2 – while even thinner Airmail paper weighs 35 g/m^2. Few people use the other extreme of the grade range – the 100 g/m^2 paper used for top quality work. A good quality typing paper has a slightly sized or glazed surface which is not very absorbent and stands up well to erasures and handling. There is a wide range of colours available but as a general rule white is used. Paper which contains recycled material is not as white as that made from other material.

Quantities

Typing paper is often sold in packs of 50–100 sheets but these are generally much more expensive in terms of cost per sheet than buying it by the ream. A ream of typing paper contains 500 sheets.

Sizes

The size of typing paper is usually based on the metric sizes (ISO) and in particular on the 'A' range. The first measurement indicates the width of the page while the second indicates its depth. The sizes most commonly used in typewriting are A4, A5 and A6. A4 measures 210 × 297 mm and it is generally used in this format – sometimes called *portrait*. A5 paper measures 148 × 210 mm (portrait) and is sometimes used *landscape*, i.e. 210 × 148 mm. A6 paper is often used for postcards and itineraries and measures 148 × 105 mm (or 105 × 148 mm). A page of A5 paper is half the size of a page of A4 paper, while a page of A6 paper is half the size of a page of A5 paper. Some firms and individuals use paper called 2/3 A4 for letters. This paper measures 210×198 mm and is folded once to fit a DL envelope. The 'A' sizes of paper are used with 'C' size envelopes – see page 32.

Some typists use the 'old' Imperial paper sizes. Of these, the sizes most commonly used are called foolscap and quarto. Unlike metric sizes, Imperial sizes are usually quoted in inches – again, the first measurement indicates the width of the paper. Foolscap measures 8×13 in while quarto measures 8×10 in.

Typing ribbons

Most electric or electronic typewriters use carbon film ribbons and there are two kinds – correctable and cover-up. Correctable ribbons should be used with lift-off ribbons while cover-up, as the name implies, have to be covered to effect a correction. In the interests of economy many typists use *multistrike* ribbons which, while not producing the quality of correctable ribbons, enable more key impacts to be obtained per ribbon. Multistrike ribbons are of the cover-up type – but not all cover-up ribbons are multistrike. Manual machines often use cotton or nylon ribbons – the latter being of superior quality. There are carbon film ribbons available for most manual machines.

MISCELLANEOUS

Dates

Dates are always produced in the order day, month, year and both the day and the year should be produced as a figure, e.g. 16 December 1983. Some authorities accept the longer months presented in their abbreviated form, while others accept the year abbreviated as indicated below.

Abbreviated months – Jan, Feb, Aug, Sept, Oct, Nov, Dec.
Abbreviated years –the apostrophe (') takes the place of the first 2 figures
    e.g. '84 (1984).

Dates may be produced using standard or open punctuation consistent with the rest of the material in which they are produced. Acceptable conventions in *open punctuation* are 16 July 1984 or 16th July 1984. Acceptable conventions in *standard punctuation* are 5 May 1984, 5th May, 1984 or 5 May, 1984.

Capital letters

When material is produced in capital letters it is usual to leave one space between each word, for example:

A DAY TO REMEMBER

Some authorities accept headings produced in capitals to have 2 spaces between each word, for example:

A MAN FOR ALL SEASONS

Spaced capitals

When material is produced in spaced capitals leave 3 spaces between each word, for example:

D R I V I N G   I N   H E A V Y   R A I N

If material follows a heading produced in spaced capitals on the same line leave 2 spaces after the last word produced in spaced capitals, for example:

Y O U R   G U A R A N T E E   is our good name.

Underscoring

When material has to be underscored on a manual typewriter, back-space to the start of the material to be underscored and type an underscored line the length of the material. Any spaces between words should also be underscored. Do not turn up before underscoring. Many electronic type-writers will automatically underscore material as it is produced, while a word processor can be instructed to underscore material – see the manual for your machine in each case. Some examination authorities do not accept the underscoring of initial or final punctuation marks, for example

<u>Half time interval</u>

<u>"How does it work?</u>"

Numbers

Numbers may be produced using standard or open punctuation. When using *open punctuation*, 4 figure number should be produced without a space between the thousands and hundreds, e.g. 5430, 9870 in general material. Five figure numbers and upwards should be produced in groups of 3 figures from the right with a space between each group, e.g. 10 800, 230 000, 1 989 790. *In column work*, all numbers should be produced in this way if the columns are to be totalled. When using *standard punctuation*, all numbers over 999 are produced in groups of 3 figures from the right with a comma (with no space either side) separating each group of 3 figures, e.g. 1,100, 20,500, 189,000, 11,450,500. *Years* are *never* punctuated no matter what the style of presentation, e.g. 1914.

Use of words or figures

In general material, when typing *cardinal numbers* (numbers indicating how many) the numbers between 1 and 9 may be produced as words or figures and those from 10 upwards as figures. Some authorities require the figure '1' to be produced as a word and all other numbers to be produced as figures. If you decide to produce all numbers as figures you should observe the following:

'One' should always be produced as a word unless indicating a section in a page, e.g. *The lists were given on pages 1–4.*

Sentences should always begin with a word and not a figure, e.g. *Five hours passed before he arrived.*

Dates should always be typed as figures – both day and year, e.g. *6 July 1984.*

Ordinal numbers indicate position, e.g. *1st (first), 3rd (third).* They may be produced as words or figures.

No matter what system you adopt you must be consistent within each exercise.

Spacing after punctuation marks

There are several acceptable conventions. The one used in the examples in this book is universally acceptable. *Leave one space* after a comma, colon or semi-colon. *Leave 2 spaces* after everything else – full stop, exclamation mark or question mark. When using full stops in *standard punctuation* leave no space after full stops within abbreviations and type a comma after the final stop in one abbreviation and the next group (if any), e.g. *B.Sc., F.R.S.A.* All abbreviations should be followed by a full stop. e.g. *Enc., Hon. Sec.*, etc.

When using open punctuation all non-essential punctuation, such as full stops and commas used in connection with abbreviations, is omitted. Essential punctuation required to punctuate sentences and phrases is included. When using standard punctuation all punctuation normally applying to correct English usage is included. Both standard and open punctuation are commercially acceptable provided that their usage is consistent within a particular piece of work. Mixtures of standard and open punctuation are not normally acceptable to examination authorities.

For the production of all units of measurement using standard or open punctuation see my *Mastering Keyboarding.*

Lines of type per page

When using the standard 6 lines per inch found on most typewriters there are:

70 lines of type down a sheet of A4 paper (210×297 mm);
50 lines of type down a sheet of A4 paper (297×210 mm);
35 lines of type down a sheet of A5 paper (210×148 mm);
50 lines of type down a sheet of A5 paper (148×210 mm).

When using 8 lines per inch there are:

94 lines of type down a sheet of A4 paper (210×297 mm);
66 lines of type down a sheet of A4 paper (297×210 mm);
47 lines of type down a sheet of A5 paper (210×148 mm);
66 lines of type down a sheet of A5 paper (148×210 mm).

Although the most commonly used typewriting paper sizes are measured in metric units, typewriters themselves are built around Imperial measurements. Typeface sizes are described in terms of 1/10, 1/12 and 1/15 of an inch while the number of lines of type are described as being 6 or 8 lines per inch. As a rough conversion it is usual to consider than 1 inch is 25 mm and that $\frac{1}{2}$ inch is 13 mm.

Characters across a page

When using 10 pitch (pica) there are 82 characters across a sheet of A4 paper (210 x 297 mm) or a sheet of A5 paper (210 x 148 mm) (landscape). There are 59 characters across a sheet of A5 paper (148 x 210 mm) (portrait).

When using 12 pitch (elite) there are 99 characters across a sheet of A4 paper (210 x 297 mm) or a sheet of A5 paper (210 x 148 mm) (landscape). There are 70 characters across a sheet of A5 paper (148 x 210 mm) (portrait).

When using 15 pitch (micro) there are 123 characters across a sheet of A4 paper (210 x 297 mm) or a sheet of A5 paper (210 x 148 mm) (landscape). There are 88 characters across a sheet of A5 paper (148 x 210 mm) (portrait).

Printers

If you are using a word processor or a microcomputer and you want printed copy, known as *hard copy* you will need a printer. Printers which print from left to right only, like a manual typewriter, are said to be *uni-directional*. Printers which print from left to right and then 'backwards' from right to left are said to be *bi-directional*. The most efficient printers are those which find the shortest route through a piece of work and only move as far back on the printing line as is necessary to reach the start of the next line. Such printers are said to be *logic-seeking*.

There are basically 5 kinds of printers in use; single element (golf ball, daisywheel or thimble), dot matrix, thermal, ink jet and laser.

INDEX